Elephants, lions & eagles

Elephants, lions & eagles

A journey through African football

Filippo Maria Ricci

WSC Books Ltd
17a Perseverance Works, 38 Kingsland Road, London E2 8DD
www.wsc.co.uk
info@wsc.co.uk

ISBN 9780954013493

Cover design by Doug Cheeseman
Cover photo by Alistair Berg – www.alistairberg.com
Printed and bound by Biddles Ltd, Kings Lynn, UK

Contents

Foreword

by Patrick Mboma

African football is particularly close to my heart and it isn't hard to understand why. Every time people talk about the subject, conjuring up the great exploits of the past, debating topical issues (players, teams, federations, institutions) or assessing future prospects, I always listen carefully. Comparing my personal experience with that of others enriches my life from day to day. My personal culture is the result of a mingling of international experiences and the same can be said of my footballing culture. Which is why my love of the game is so special. Though football for me is the king of sports, there are moments in which, despite my experience of different lifestyles, I feel slightly naive. Paradoxically, this happens most when the talk turns to Africa. There are big differences between people from the countries of the Maghreb and those from southern Africa, between Muslims and Christians, between English-speakers and French-speakers, between this racial group and that. I still can't get over how many talents Africa possesses, what a rich nursery it is for the game and how much interest our football attracts.

There comes a day when a meeting with a person, chance or planned, ties you to him or her forever. A sentence strikes you and sticks indelibly in your memory. A way of behaving impresses you and you realise that, in that moment, something is starting to gel. I don't know how or why I met Filippo Ricci – for that matter I don't know how or why I met my wife Guila or my manager Pierre Lechantre or my friend George Weah. I have to say though that I was totally won over by Filippo and his knowledge of Africa. Of African football, that is.

The person that comes across in this book is a person keen to understand mentalities, habits and customs. All we can do is to stand back in admiration at the passion that has motivated Filippo over the years. I love Filippo's attention to detail and his careful description of events.

I ended up wondering whether my friend Filippo's meeting with African football wasn't a stroke of fortune. It is a great pleasure for me to see the merits of our sport celebrated and the characteristics that make it attractive for the world explained. The way the author distances himself from events, the precision of the information he supplies and his analysis of phenomena such as the diaspora of African footballers all allow us to understand why football is so popular among us Africans.

Patrick Mboma

Patrick Mboma retired in the summer of 2005 and decided to continue his career in football as an agent. Born in Cameroon 1970, he grew up in France. In the course of his 12-year career, he played in France (Chateauroux, Metz, Paris Saint-Germain), Italy (Cagliari, Parma), England (Sunderland) and Japan (Gamba Osaka, Tokyo Verdy, Vissel Kobe). For the Cameroon national side, he played twice in the World Cup (1998 and 2002), four times in the African Cup of Nations (1998, 2000, 2002, 2004) winning two, and won a gold medal at the Sydney Olympics in 2000. In the same year he was voted African Footballer of the Year.

Introduction

The first African Cup of Nations was played in 1957. Four countries entered the tournament, which dropped to three when South Africa were expelled for wanting to field an all-white team. In the same year, the journalist Ryszard Kapuscinski was sent to Africa by PASP, the Polish national press agency. In the course of 40 years' correspondence, he was to describe the continent better than anyone. He argued that Africa does not exist, that there are at least four Africas: northern, western, eastern and southern. 'The continent is too large to describe. It is a veritable ocean, a varied, immensely rich cosmos. Only with the greatest simplification, for the sake of convenience can we say "Africa". In reality, except as a geographical appellation, Africa does not exist.'

This concept also applies to football. In North Africa it is fragmented, rowdy and edgy; in west Africa – Cameroon, Nigeria, Ghana, Senegal – it is the version we are used to seeing at the African Cup of Nations, with flying tackles and shots from ridiculous distance, strong men and dodgy goalkeepers, talent, skill and ingenuity all mixed in; in the Horn of Africa it is in decline; in southern Africa it is as intricate as a forest, and South Africa in particular is a novelty that defies categorisation. In the rest of the world, though, we talk solely in terms of African football, randomly simplifying, condensing and cramming. But, as if to confirm this Africa United concept, whenever African footballers meet up on pitches round the world, they greet each other and embrace and talk. As if they all came from the same country. Maybe because they share similar stories and experiences of hope, suffering, hunger, nostalgia and optimism.

This book's Italian title was *Scusate Il Ritardo* – Sorry for the Delay. Africa has taken 80 years to organise a World Cup, 60 to reach the quarter-finals. Whether it can reach the semi-finals and the final, we will have to wait and see. The title speaks for me and for the book itself; it speaks for African football and for chances never taken; it speaks for the continent, where delays are an art form, not a lack of manners. This book discusses African football and my experiences following it, some in Africa, others in Europe. From Rome's Parioli neighbourhood in 1993 to Ghana in 2006. In between, there are glimpses of the Africa that does not exist but that has dominated my life as an African football expert for so many years. With an activist's passion, I have written articles, gathered data, published books and edited picture card collections to try, in my own small way, to help African football build itself a historical memory – something which it had hardly contemplated itself.

I wish to thank my Italian publisher, who welcomed the idea of this journey with enthusiasm, and Tommaso Pellizzari, who kicked off the project. For the English edition, I have to thank Andy Lyons, the editor of *When Saturday Comes*, whom I first met at the African Cup of Nations in 1996, and his colleagues Mike Ticher, Ed Upright and Richard Guy. John Irving provided the translation from the original Italian – as a Carlisle fan who decided to live in Bra (Piedmont) and write about 'slow food', John was the best possible person to understand and translate the moods of an Italian who fell in love with African football.

I am also grateful to Patrick Mboma, for the kindness and passion with which he accepted my idea of inverting our roles – a footballer writing for a journalist; to my brother Checco for his encouragement, continuous support and precious advice; to Benedetta, whose hand was asked during an African Cup of Nations many years ago, and since then has been a great travelling companion, sharing everything with patience, love and enthusiasm.

FMR

1. Profession: African football reporter

I don't really know what to expect. I park my battered scooter on the pavement on the other side of the road, I look up at the green, white and orange flag and I walk into the *art nouveau* building on Via Spallanzani in Rome's Salario neighbourhood. Down a short gravel pathway, up a flight of stairs and I am inside. A lift in front of me, a closed door on my right and an open door on my left. I proceed into a large room, with a huge glass-topped table and patent leather armchairs with fabric-upholstered chairs on either side. People waiting, people chatting, people reading the papers.

I look for someone I can talk to and I come across Diabate. He's the telephone operator, the heart and soul and driving force of the Ivory Coast embassy in Rome. Tall, self-confident with bright, lively eyes, hurried in his movements, he takes his job seriously. He behaves like someone who spends part of every day defending his personal space from intrusions: unsolvable hassles; questions that require long, drawn-out answers; wearisome requests. Readiness to help has a price. I explain to Diabate why I am here. I'm looking for newspapers. His eyes are asking me 'So why don't you go to the news stand?' but he listens without a word.

I am looking for newspapers because I want to find fresh African football stories and news to write about in the Bologna-based Italian football weekly *Guerin Sportivo*. What a brilliant idea! Diabate struggles to keep his cool. He adores football, it's his life. Football and music (in his free time he is a DJ for a Rome commercial radio station, Radio Città Futura). And here's this listless white guy coming in, asking him if he can read the local papers. 'Ask me, never mind the papers!' he blurts. We start to talk. People are waiting and the phone's ringing, but Diabate has no time for them or for calls from who knows where. No one complains.

He takes me into the waiting room. Neatly arranged, under the glass top of the table, are the sports pages of *Le Jour*, the major Abidjan daily. The rest of the paper gets passed round from hand to hand, but not the sports pages. They are a precious item and woe betide anyone who creases or stains or tears them. The paper may be three days old, but it is a real find for me. The concept of topicality has a different meaning in Africa but I've no problems in adapting to that. It won't be the last time. I note down some items of interesting news, I spend half an hour with Diabate and I leave as happy as can be.

Geed up by my success, I walk confidently into the next building along, the Moroccan embassy. What an anticlimax! 'Who sent you? What are you looking for? The *Guerin Sportivo*? Moroccan newspapers?' This north African indifference comes as a shock. I'll get hardened to it but, for the moment, I make no headway and leave. My unwillingness to tackle them head-on makes them all the more suspicious. Slightly crestfallen, I go back to my scooter and decide to give Ghana a go. The embassy is on a posh road, inside one of Rome's biggest parks, Villa Ada. I walk through the black gate. The downstairs door is open for anyone who just needs a visa. Upstairs is closed. I ring the bell.

After a long wait, they let me in. I explain why I'm there and they ask me to wait some more. A few minutes later, I'm asked to go up an imposing flight of stairs. Halfway up I'm met by an immense portrait of Kwame Nkrumah, the legendary, much loved, unmatched first president of independent Ghana – one of the fathers of modern Africa. At the top of the stairs, a very kind clerk awaits me. She listens to me, goes off and comes back with a sizeable parcel of papers; she even lets me use a photocopier. The *Daily Graphic*, the *Ghanaian Chronicle*, the *Mirror*, the *Independent* – the names echo those of British newspapers as do structure and layout, with the sport at the end, starting from the back page.

Neri, oggi e domani (Black, Today and Tomorrow), *neri* (black) being a pun on *ieri* (yesterday). *Guerin Sportivo* has built its history on jokey headlines: this was the first to be thought up for news from Africa gathered through the embassies in Rome. They publish a page with seven 'bullets' of varying lengths – all dedicated to Ghana, given the abundance of news I'm able to gather at the country's embassy. From the sacking of the German coach Otto Pfister after Ghana were knocked out of the 1994 World Cup qualifying groups to the attempts by the president of the football federation to staunch the exodus of young players to Europe – two subjects that are still topical – to sponsorship and exotic donations. A goat, 200 eggs and 50,000 cedis (the local currency, about £100 at the exchange rate of the time) for Hearts of Oak, one of Accra's top teams. A strip, 20 balls and 20 pairs of boots for Voradep, a team from Ho in southern Ghana. A strip and three cartons of milk, again for the Hearts. More news from Ghana follows in the next week's *Guerin*: the launch of the football pools and a 100 per cent increase in the price of match tickets. As the weeks go by, the horizon broadens.

Access to the South African embassy was impossible. Apartheid had just come to an end but the atmosphere in the country was still tense. The newspapers in the embassies of Guinea, Zambia and other countries were too old, and the offices of Nigeria and Cameroon were always busy and disorganised. But I came across more interesting material in Senegal and Mali.

That was a memorable date for me, April 14, 1993. My first taste of African football in the national press. A passion that has never waned. At times overpowering and exhausting, partly stifled when I moved to London, but never entirely extinguished, always ready to explode again. Three things led me down this road. I wanted to be a journalist and, since no one in Italy was covering African football permanently, it seemed like a good Trojan horse, a chance to start writing at a certain level. A year earlier, in March 1992, the 18th African Cup of Nations had been staged in Senegal. It was the first to attract journalists, scouts, experts and wheeler-dealers from north of the Mediterranean in any number. Even Arrigo Sacchi, who had become manager of Italy the previous November, had travelled to Dakar. It was a reconnaissance mission that led him to join the multitude who were claiming that 'African football will be the football of 2000'. If Maestro Arrigo says so, it must be true, I thought. An investment worth making, I told myself by way of encouragement.

The third reason for my passion was a family connection. The fourth of my five brothers, Domenico, nicknamed Chicco, had just come back from Zaire (today the Democratic Republic of Congo, previously the Belgian Congo). He had gone there with his wife and, among other things, had achieved some success as coach of Bilima, the third team in the capital, Kinshasa. Amid general surprise and several non-sporting ups and downs (for the team and for my brother), he took them to the final of the 1985 African Champions Cup, losing to FAR of Rabat in Morocco. Over the years, before returning home with a wonderful little daughter and a huge, virtually empty suitcase, Chicco had sent home photographs from Zaire. One of them showed him standing beside the bench during a Bilima match, smartly dressed in a shirt and tie and a cream-coloured suit – a white dot in a sea of black. Back in Italy, he started working as an agent, and Senegal 1992 marked his baptism in the job. He was a real believer in Africa and African football. A love affair that was sincere and monogamous, faithful and absolute. I followed hot on his heels.

One hot afternoon in Rome, less than three weeks after my first 'tour of Africa', I receive a phone call: the plane carrying the Zambian national team to play in a crucial World Cup qualifying match has crashed into the Atlantic off the coast of Gabon. There are no survivors. I rush to the embassy, hoping to find someone there. The offices, on the third floor of a building in Rome's Prati quarter, are full of people, all clamouring for news: who was on the plane and who wasn't, what happened exactly and how? Information trickles in slowly. A clerk calls me into a room. 'If you're interested, we've got Kalusha Bwalya's number. Maybe we could call him.' Bwalya was the star of the team, but he wasn't on the plane. He was to travel separately from Holland, where he was played for PSV Eindhoven, and meet up with his team-mates later.

Five years earlier, at the Seoul Olympics, he had scored a hat-trick for Zambia against Italy, with the former Juventus keeper Stefano Tacconi in goal. It was an unforgettable debacle for our national team. We called Bwalya and he gave us a bit of first-hand information. Some of it was alarming. The plane, an army transporter, was old and the worse for wear. There were 30 people dead, 18 of them players. The team was no more. Kalusha wasn't crying, but he was desperately sad. All at once, he'd lost at least a dozen very dear friends with whom he had been playing since he was a kid.

The crash turned out to be an absurd, maybe avoidable, tragedy. It was followed by long and useless enquiries (the Zambian government took ten years to complete the first report on the event) and international controversy (Zambia blamed Gabon for delays in the rescue operation and bad management of the enquiry). There was very little compensation for the families of the victims – not a penny from CAF, the Confederation of

African Football. Just days after my first experience of Africa, here I was, catapulted into a story in its own way emblematic of African football's lack of means, of the tragic turn that events often take on the continent. A year later, I experienced the other side of the coin, a vital explosion of great human resources and character, of great inner strength. With a rebuilt team, plus Bwalya, the *Chipolopolo* (Copper Bullets) reached the final of the African Cup of Nations in Tunisia, losing to Nigeria. It was a sporting miracle.

In the years since then, I have spent many hours at the African Cup of Nations with Kalusha, and I celebrated with him in Zurich in 2004 when South Africa was chosen to host the 2010 World Cup. He was there to present a testimonial for Mandela and his country. I invited him to the bar and offered to buy him a drink. 'What do you fancy?' 'Twelve beers,' he replied. He was with a group of friends and he did not want to disappoint them.

Scent of peace in Ivory Coast

The national team's coach, Frenchman Philippe Troussier, has given Abdoulaye Traore, the star of ASEC and the Ivory Coast, a large bottle of perfume as a token of his friendship. Traore, nicknamed Ben Badi, had announced that he would never wear the national team shirt again as long as Troussier was coach. The local press gave the peace offering massive coverage.

Guerin Sportivo, April 1993

2. Miracle in Ouaga

Very dark and very hot. That's the first impression I have from the steps of the plane on landing in Ouagadougou, the capital of Burkina Faso. Public lighting is expensive and there's no reason to waste such energy on the runway. The heat grabs you by the throat, but it's dry, drawn in by the *harmattan*, the boiling wind that comes off the Sahel desert. Waiting in the queue in the hangar reserved for customs, health procedures and baggage collection, I keep a tight hold of my yellow vaccination card. It is a precious document. The queue moves slowly. I am impatient and look around for signals.

I see a clerk checking the vaccination cards and putting the ones he considers irregular into a pile, which grows by the minute. The owners of the cards are moved to a room where they are brusquely injected for yellow fever. I've always had a phobia of needles and I feel myself growing paler and paler. The severe health inspector, a man with only one eye, chucks my card onto the pile of the reprobates for vaccination. I start waving my arms and try to grab my document back from the untidy pile. Without getting the clerk's back up, I point to the stamp of the health unit in Rome. He shakes his head. 'I can't see anything,' he says. So I shift the document and he pauses for a moment to weigh up the new information through his good eye. '*Ça va*, go through.' I start breathing again. I take a quick glance into the impromptu clinic and feel a surge of euphoria. I'd never have survived in there.

It is the start of February 1998, I am here for the African Cup of Nations, my third in a row, the greatest experience ever, the journey that added real roots to my passion for African football, a passion born in Rome and developed in Tunisia, Morocco and South Africa. Black Africa is a long, long way from the Maghreb – part of the Arabic area of north Africa – and in no way comparable with South Africa, a country that is a law unto itself within the continent. My first encounter was devastating, but in a positive sense. Burkina Faso, by definition the 'country of upright men', is a heart-rending place. The air, the people, the slowness that turns to calm, the serenity, the positivity, the smiles, the industriousness, the organisation. The Afro-reggae of Black Showman provides the background music for a whole city. The temperature is a steady 45 degrees Celsius and matches are played at 3pm for fear that the lights will go off after dark. Long journeys across a city that embraced me and welcomed me with great politeness while I improvised my own Ramadan; generous breakfasts at the OK Inn, my hotel, and all-meat dinners at the Eau Vive, a restaurant run by nuns; in between, water and bananas and, to end the day, a beer at the *Festa dell'Unità*, the Cup of Nations village that we had nicknamed after the annual festival of the former Italian Communist Party's daily newspaper.

'In Burkina there's no money, so you've got to go out and earn it,' a taxi driver told me. Which is why everyone's on the move. From six in the morning to midnight, the streets are in ferment, thousands of people dashing backwards and forwards, on foot, on bikes, in taxis and cars and lorries, but above all on their mobylettes, scooter-like vehicles that are the true symbol of the nation. Even the stretcher used to take injured players off the field during the African Cup of Nations is pulled by a mobylette, and during the opening ceremony there's a display by the Mobylette Virtuosos, women who perform incredible slaloms with huge baskets balanced on their heads. Ouagadougou, a million inhabitants, five districts, 28 sectors and a dozen cinemas – and kilometre upon kilometre of scooter and bicycle lanes. A nation on the move with a head full of thoughts and a never-ending supply of questions.

Burkina Faso was the third-poorest country in Africa at the time of my visit. Landlocked, clutched tightly in the embrace of six bordering nations, it makes up for its lack of the facilities we take for granted with other resources. Human resources, above all, since the country was left in dire straits when France withdrew in 1958. Known as Upper Volta until 1983, it became Burkina Faso at the will of Thomas Sankara, a young Marxist revolutionary who held power for just over three years before being assassinated by his friend and comrade Blaise Compaoré. As president, Compaoré inaugurated and followed the 1998 Cup of Nations and even played a charity match, all smiles and pats on the back, against the Cameroon All Stars: Roger Milla, goalkeeper Joseph-Antoine Bell and the former Indomitable Lions manager Claude Le Roy. The

Cameroonians wore the jerseys of Paris St-Germain, where Le Roy was coaching at the time.

It was Sankara who explained: 'Burkina means noble, upright. Faso refers to an organised community. Burkina Faso is thus a nation that advocates integrity, nobility and rectitude.' He is buried in a tomb without a plaque just outside the centre of Ouaga, to this day a place of pilgrimage for followers and believers. Coloured stickers of the former army officer in his beret are still prominently displayed on many of the scooters in Ouaga. This African Che Guevara has entered people's hearts and his three years in government ensured he would not be forgotten. Sankara chose the Renault 4 as his presidential car and to this day the model that was the symbol of hippies throughout Europe in the Seventies is still the *Burkinabés'* favourite. Sankara fought successfully against corruption and the state's squandering of resources, but also against desertification and childhood illnesses. He promised and often guaranteed free housing and was concerned about the plight of women, who are still seriously discriminated against. The western world, however, frowned upon Sankara because he was a friend of Libya's Colonel Gaddafi and the Soviet Union.

Fifteen years after the brutal overthrow of Sankara, I sensed that traces of real socialism lingered in Burkina Faso in the way taxi drivers treated their passengers. In their Renault 4s – and 5s and 14s and 18s – the taxi drivers of Ouaga were among the few to benefit from the staging of the Cup of Nations. Journalists tended to follow set routes at set times. And since everyone has a family to keep, why not share out the work? After a couple of days, my daily schedule and that of a number of my colleagues in Ouaga had been worked out and organised by the taxi drivers themselves – every time I left somewhere, one of them was waiting for me. In the morning at the OK Inn, my hotel in the suburbs with a swimming pool full of soil and seaweed, the nightspot of the *Ghanéennes*, a derogatory term used to describe sex workers of every rank, and its smiling, friendly good-humoured staff. Later on, at the Hotel Indépendance, the focal point of the African Cup of Nations, where the press office and the operational heart of the event were situated. At the 4 Août, the stadium made over with a fresh coat of paint and an electronic scoreboard, but otherwise very basic, the heat oozing from its incandescent terraces. Then, of an evening, at the Eau Vive, the French nuns' restaurant where we went to eat, with its well kept garden, its very expensive market where they sold delightful tablecloths sewed by the nuns, and the room where children drew and played by day. Then, last of all, at the *Festa dell'Unità*, with its central stage for dancing contests and bars and shops, where the day came to an end.

I've no idea how they did it, as they never asked any questions, but the taxi drivers parked outside these regular haunts of ours and would always decide in which car we should travel. Even if there were occasional changes in schedule in the course of a day, the first and last ride of the day were always with the same two taxis. If, for some unforeseen reason, I had to change my schedule, it was never a problem. The drivers knew that I would reappear in one of the usual places and off we would go again. The first ride of the day, from the OK Inn to the Hotel Indépendance, had been contracted to a jovial character with a face lined with ritual scars. Our brief route always included a pit stop for a petrol refill. I used to pay a piddling sum as an advance on the fare. The taxi wouldn't have gone very far with such a tiny amount of petrol but it seemed to be the rule never to invest more than a few *céfas* (CFAs or Central African francs) at a time and to stop very frequently, to refuel.

The highlight was the night ride. The dark blue R4 was driven by an old timer who, given the late shift, was suitably dressed in a light windcheater. True, the temperature in Ouaga never dropped below 30 degrees Celsius but the darkness must have made him feel shivery. When I climbed into the car, he would lean back against the door and make a half-turn to look me over. There was no danger of his not seeing anything on the road: the R4 never went faster than 20 kilometres an hour, and to do the six kilometres from the centre to the OK Inn took at least half an hour. It was important to look at each other in the eye because every evening he would launch a new topic of conversation. The emigration of *Burkinabés* (in those days they used to go to Villa Literno in Campania, southern Italy, to pick tomatoes), racism in Europe, the Burkina Faso economy, politics and corruption in Africa, prostitution and Aids, education and so on. Everything except football. The talk would carry on for another half hour after we'd arrived in the hotel car park. It was he who explained to me the functioning of 'real communism' as applied to the rides of journalists in Ouaga.

This desire to talk, ask questions, enquire, find out more and argue was common to many other people. It often happened that a waiter would ask for a private audience. 'Can I talk to you?' (the tone of the request was always grave and serious). 'Sure, what about?' Topics for discussion were always complex and interesting, but there wasn't always time to develop them properly. 'In your opinion, should I go to Italy to pick tomatoes?' was one of the questions I was asked point-blank. But it was asked politely and with good manners – not to mention great trust in my opinion.

When, in 1994, CAF chose Burkina Faso to organise the 1998 African Cup of Nations, the announcement was received with surprise and concern. It was commonly held that the country was incapable of organising, staging, hosting and managing an event that, with the World Cup coming up the same year, would attract observers and journalists from all over the world. What a lack of respect that turned out to be. Albeit with infinitely inferior means at their disposal, the *Burkinabés* outclassed the self-important organisers in Mandela's South Africa, where the Cup had been staged two years earlier, technologically, socially and in terms of atmosphere. The *Festa dell'Unità* was a simple, magical place: though it was always packed with people, you could go there with your computer and camera and still feel safe. There were plastic tables and chairs and something of the friendly mood of a village fête.

Ultimately, it was the *Burkinabés* who were ripped off. In Ouaga they were expecting huge crowds but they had to make do with a thousand or so football insiders: reporters, agents, scouts and the like. Not much of a show and, worse still, not much business. Africans were conspicuous by their absence. Three of the nations bordering Burkina had qualified for the tournament and everybody was looking forward to a big influx of supporters. But it didn't happen. 'Compared to FESPACO, the African Cup is peanuts. There's nobody here,' was the refrain. FESPACO, the African film and television festival of Ouagadougou that came into being in 1969 as the 'Week of African Cinema', was held for the 20th time in 2007. The past few years have also seen the organisation of a theatre festival and an International Craft Show, pan-African events that attract lots of people to Ouaga. With this experience, organising the African Cup of Nations would not be a problem.

Obviously enough, the tickets at the August 4 Stadium have sold out. They actually went on sale for only a few minutes:

Oumarou Kanazoé, Burkina Faso's top businessman and chairman of the supporters' committee of the Stallions – the nickname of the national team taken from the Stallion of Yenenga, the Burkina Faso national symbol – bought 30,000 of the 35,000 tickets available *en bloc* and asked people to go to the stadium, form orderly queues and collect their match tickets for free. This had already happened before the matches against Algeria and Guinea, without rioting or fighting. The tickets cost the equivalent of £1.50 to £5. Kanazoé, the benefactor, is like a figure from a different age: he likes appearing on the TV news as he hands over wads of bank notes to players, blocks of tickets to fans or the keys for a new Mercedes to Kassoum Ouedraogo, who plays in Germany and scored the first Burkina goal against Algeria. Now expectations are mounting not only for the match but also to find out the bonus Kanazoé has promised the Stallions if they qualify for the semi-finals. In the city of cinema, they are expecting another *coup de théâtre*.

Ansa News Agency, February 18, 1998

3. The magic of the cup

The African Cup of Nations embodies not so much the football of the future as an idea of the football of the past. If modern football means stress, pressure, an overdose of television, poison and dirt, then the African Cup of Nations is like a treasured memory of happy experiences. A traditional country inn compared to a fast food joint. Ingenuousness versus cunning. A referee's blunders compared to slow-motion analysis and over-the-top television debates. Following the African Cup is still a pleasure. True, each country has its own distinctive characteristics and local difficulties – certain structural limitations may cause headaches even for regular match goers. African football officials do their best to pick up the worst European and world football has to offer, yet the Cup always manages to ensure positive sensations.

Hence as a rule – and with obvious exceptions – there are no high-security training camps at the African Cup, no bodyguards, no prearranged press conferences, no news blackouts, no players taking turns to speak to reporters and answering questions in monosyllables. For all the people involved in the tournament – players, journalists, referees, fans – the Cup of Nations is, above all, an opportunity to get together. The fact that it takes place every two years helps, of course. One tournament is not over before the qualifying rounds get under way for the next, and two years is not long enough to lose touch with people you maybe only see there. African journalists are often lucky if they can afford to make phone calls to Europe, never mind travel there, so the Cup is a great place to consolidate friendships that used to be maintained through letters, today by email – relationships with an old-fashioned flavour.

For the players, the tournament is a great opportunity to meet up with old friends, people they have grown up with but who have since been carried off by football. Only 31 per cent of the players at the 2006 African Cup of Nations in Egypt were registered with clubs in their own countries: 255 of the 368 present were playing abroad, mainly in

Europe but also in other African countries, in the Middle East, Asia and the Americas. The players try to arrive as soon as they can and leave as late as possible. In 2000, after Nigeria lost in the final, Nwankwo Kanu, Celestine Babayaro, Taribo West and Jay-Jay Okocha, who were at that time playing in England, Italy and France, returned to Europe ten days after the final whistle was blown. In Nigeria it is easy to disappear without trace and the chance to spend a few stress-free days at home has to be taken. Who cares if, back in Europe, they are losing their tempers or worrying or getting ready to hand out fines? There's time to think about all that later. After all, freedom has a price, and sometimes it can involve paying your club a hefty penalty in foreign currency.

In the African Cup of Nations, the competing teams all tend to stay in the same hotels. In 1998 in Ouagadougou, Burkina Faso, eight of the 16 teams were put up at Ouaga 2000, a residential centre just out of town, built for the France-Africa summit the year before: a row of houses in the middle of the desert, 350 beds and a continuous coming and going of players of different nationalities, many of whom play in the same teams in Europe. During the long breaks between matches and training sessions, the squads end up socialising, exchanging information about their team-mates and trying to impress journalists by speaking in the languages of the European countries in which they play – something that always causes a stir. They eat together and comb each others' hair and chat, whiling away the day in true transnational fashion.

The Burkinian residential centre was an exception to the general rule. Normally at the Cup of Nations, all the teams stay together in one large hotel. So you may see five South African players in the hall playing a Turkish card game, inventing a new language halfway between Zulu and Turkish. For them it is a token of distinction, proof they play in Europe, that they are successful. Talking to a journalist in Italian is like wearing a gold medal with the words 'I've made it. I can speak the language of Serie A' engraved on it.

The foyer of the chosen hotel is akin to a crowded plaza, where everyone displays their wares and tries to do business. Agents in search of new talents, journalists on the lookout for interviews, photographers selling pictures taken at the stadium or in the hall itself of players, journalists and fans, girls selling shirts and fans clamouring for autographs, photos or even shirts from their idols.

The players lounge about on the many sofas. It is here you realise you are in a different world. Light years away from Italian training grounds such as Milanello (AC Milan), Trigoria (AS Roma), Formello (Lazio) or Appiano Gentile (Internazionale) in Italy, or Carrington (Manchester United), London Colney (Arsenal) and Cobham (Chelsea) in England, where you can enter only once a week for the manager's press conference. Contact is direct. If a player feels like it, he can spend a whole day with you. It is he who searches you out, to play table tennis or pass on information about his club team, or maybe to ask a quick piece of medical advice: sometimes there is a shortage of mineral salts, vitamins, bandages or blister plasters, and if someone happens to turn up from Europe, maybe they can lend a helping hand.

Referees stay in a different hotel. In these places there are fewer crowds, but no lack of photographers, every self-respecting African referee having to go home with a few snaps of his African Cup of Nations. If the referees find out you are a journalist, they may ask you what you think about their performances – like the footballers themselves. What follows is an impromptu slow-motion replay in words, with referees commenting on the matches, admitting mistakes, apologising, trying to explain things, politely but with passion. The fact is that you see mistakes that are so glaringly obvious, you are forced to laugh, especially if you are neutral.

Unless the manager is especially nervy, there is no problem at the African Cup of Nations going to training sessions on the coach with the team. I remember when, as I climbed onto the Zaire coach during the 1996 tournament in South Africa, the players started singing. All together, 30 people, from the 18-year-old debutant to the ancient masseur who could have been his father or even his granddad. They gave me the shivers. I realised I was at the African Cup of Nations, that I was somewhere else. Maybe the players talk different dialects or languages, but the songs are always the same, the ones they sing in the dressing rooms or in the tunnel, to impress the opponents lined up alongside them, who, unless they are petrified, sing back in an incredible battle of sound, a foretaste of what is to come on the field.

Then there are the matches themselves. Unless they are being played in north Africa, the weather is generally very hot, but the organisers try to schedule as many matches as possible in the early afternoon to avoid games being called off due to sudden blackouts – always a possibility in

Africa. It is better to think ahead, even if that means extra hard work for the players.

When the home team is to play, the stadium opens its gates early in the morning, seven or eight hours before kick off. By 11am it is virtually full. At which point the 'happening' commences. The battle on the terraces is not about crowd formations or chants or banners. They do not have enough money here to waste on such luxuries, so they fight it out with music. To see who can play best, longest and loudest. Many supporters' bands appear on the terraces with drums, plus woodwind sections that wouldn't be out of place in a jazz club. After a cue from the band leader, they never stop. In the lead-up to the match, the repertoire can be quite varied, but during the game the Nigerian fans, for example, play the same tune over and over again, a mantra that turns into background music.

The hours leading up to the match fly by. The vendors are very well organised and offer a full range of items. Kebabs, fritters, hot dogs, sandwiches, fruit, fried vegetables. At north African grounds they go by with flasks of coffee and receptacles that look like bagpipes filled with water and a cup to drink out of. One cup for the whole stadium, naturally. I was reminded of the stands in Italian stadiums in the Seventies, when the *curve* were filled with dishes and crockery of all shapes and sizes – not to mention the women in Rome who used to take trays of lasagne into the Tribuna Tevere, the main grandstand at the Stadio Olimpico.

If there are no bands, the organisers see that the crowd is kept happy. In Africa it is not only majorettes who take the field. What they really like is a DJ with two decks and a powerful sound system, speakers turned to the terraces. Music at full throttle with thousands of people dancing. Football is a party and the brightest colours win. The only similarity with Europe is the fans' hostility to the police, who receive the same acrimonious welcome as at our grounds every weekend.

Music is a vital element in African life. You see it in the football. The teams don't play Brazilian-style *futbol bailado*, but the pre-match warm-up is more like a dance than a workout. All together, the players move to the same rhythm, perfectly co-ordinated as if they were being directed by a choreographer to the sound of music. Maybe it is not the most orthodox method to warm up, but who cares? What counts is movement, harmony, sensations – a sense of unity demonstrated when the players pray together in the centre of the pitch. All of them, some youngsters who have embraced different religions, in a circle with the pastor, the player-preacher who guides the group. Every team has one.

At the end of the game, they all climb into the coach to go back to the hotel for a shower. This is what teams are accustomed to in Africa; normally they cannot afford a training ground with dressing rooms and showers, so from childhood onwards the players go home to get washed. In the African Cup of Nations there are also other motivations: above all, the desire to return to the comfort of the hotel, a place that becomes a second home. After showering, if things have gone well, the players go down to the foyer to talk to fans and reporters about the match.

It would be great to go to the Cup of Nations on holiday with friends, especially when it is held in one of the black African countries. If you take away the stress of having to work with sometimes fitful communications systems, demands from European news desks, inhuman deadlines, the hurry and the need to travel fast in vehicles that are not exactly high-tech, all the rest is wonderful. I went to the Cup of Nations with some friends once. It was my debut, in Tunisia in 1994. My travelling companions were a bankruptcy receiver, a Calabrian urban anthropologist, a socialist DJ and a restaurateur nicknamed Giampiero (after the Italian football commentator Giampiero Galeazzi) Quai (after Jamiroquai) on account of his elegant, easy-going look: Adidas Gazelle trainers, grey suit, fez.

They had fun noting the loose morals of Serie A scouts and enjoyed the matches, the balmy weather and the comfort of hotels that were at once luxurious and cheap. Without bothering about tickets ('All you have to do to get into the stadium here is to carry a diary with you,' said an Italian agent. 'Just look important and no one will stop you'), practising the art of vaulting to reach the best seats and, in typically brazen Roman fashion, sitting next to Carlo Ancelotti, then the right-hand man of Italy's national manager Arrigo Sacchi, talking about the match with him and even scrawling in his notebook.

In Burkina Faso there was a colourful group of blond Swedish spectators on holiday, and in Ghana I came across some English people. Often the matches are nothing to write home about and the football's old-fashioned, a bit stale, short on ideas. But the game is only a pretext. It is the Cup as a whole that counts, for everybody concerned. For us who write about it and for those who play for it.

4. Missing in Maputo

I needed Africa for me to complete my first Panini picture card album. I've always had a love-hate relationship with picture cards. It all began when I was about two and I enjoyed stealing albums from my brother Checco, who is eight years older than me, and throwing them out of the window of our fifth-floor house. They tell me I used to roar with laughter when I did that. The problem continued at primary school when, despite many attempts, I never managed to finish a single football collection. I have always felt a bit ashamed of myself because of that.

Towards the end of 1994, I received a call from Modena. It was Daniela, a close friend of mine who worked at Panini. 'They'd like to do a collection on African football, and I've mentioned your name. Do you feel up to it? They'll be in touch.' Actually, I did not feel up to it. Where would I find the photos? How could I collect data that was virtually non-existent? How could I hope to live up to the expectations of the most famous of all picture card companies? Then the dreaded phone call arrived and I was summoned to Modena. It is a city I know very well. Checco, the brother to whom I am closest, the brother who patiently put the pieces of his album back together again after I had torn them apart, had lived there for years. He used to complete his albums, my big brother.

Panini, Via Emilio Po, Modena. As a kid, I never understood that strange address. A first name and the name of a river? That was the address where you had to send requests for missing cards or to claim prizes, the address that was on every single packet and every card, one of the first addresses to leave a mark on my memory. The Panini offices were a building with a flat roof, that had once been modern but wasn't any more. Inside, through a glass door, an unmistakable smell: welcoming, reassuring. The cards travel miles, they go all over the world, but they never lose their smell. On the first floor, a fussy bureaucrat was waiting for me, on edge and hard to please. 'Things aren't looking good,' I thought. He showed me an agreement that looked very good financially but was also packed with small print – demands, penalties and deadlines that, judging from my first experiences of Africa, I reckoned would be impossible to meet. Then in came Arrigo Beltrami, the top dog, the man who for 30 years had been churning out thousands of Panini collections on everything from football to dolls, from animals to superheroes. He was something of a superhero himself, a sticker production guru with the Fifimatic, the machine invented in the Sixties by Umberto Panini, one of the founders of the company, but for me simply the dad of Marco, a friend of mine in Modena.

Beltrami was grumpy and incredibly demanding but unbeatable at his job – elegant, cool and detached. The Panini family had sold the company a few years before. It had ended up first in very unsteady hands, then in receivership, but now it was back on its feet again. Beltrami had always worked there, first with the family management and then with the American-style executives who understood nothing but earned loads of cash and had wild and wonderful ideas. He was a real character, Beltrami, a tough guy but also ready to see the funny side when I turned up with photos of footballers playing billiards (we had to turn the informal snap into head-and-shoulders shots for an album) or wearing denim jackets instead of jerseys (I had yet to discover the magic of photo retouching). He also understood the practical difficulties I came up against in Africa or Turkey (in Modena they always used to give me the trickiest markets) and acted accordingly, always letting me off the hook.

A couple of years after that meeting I found myself in Cairo, in the huge offices of Al-Ahram, one of the giants of Arab publishing and owners of the most important daily newspaper in Egypt with a circulation of millions. I was there to gather material for the album on the Egyptian first division. They took me to the photo archive, a large room whose walls were lined with huge wooden cabinets full of drawers. They contained the 'archive', thousands of photographs piled together randomly in no alphabetical or chronological order. I was desperate. I couldn't make head or tail of the mess, never mind produce an album out of it. Sinking into a sofa, the give of which captured my state of mind perfectly, I called Beltrami. I didn't know what to tell him, and I was afraid of how he might react. 'Don't worry, take everything you can, get an idea of where we can find what's missing, and we'll sort everything out at this end, you'll see,' he said. And he was right.

At my first meeting with Panini, we established how we would go about compiling our first African football collection and how long it would take. It had to come out in time for the subsequent Cup, scheduled for the beginning of 1996 in South Africa. There were 316 cards: the 16 competing teams (15 players each, group shot plus flag), the three biggest teams that had failed to qualify (eight players plus group shot), nine all-time greats and photos of the four cities and the four stadiums that were to host the tournament. So, 316 cards, no one to swap them with, only a few places where I could buy the photographs – it seemed like mission impossible. Another problem was that the collection had to be assembled while the qualifying rounds were still under way, and results so far were suggesting that teams such as Liberia, Burkina Faso and Mozambique would qualify. Good for them, but nations such as these were going to complicate my task. The agreement was finalised in June and a month later I was off to South Africa.

In Cape Town lived Mark Gleeson, one of the two journalists in the world (the other, Frank Simon, lives in Paris) who wrote about African football in its entirety. I was about to become the third, and it was vital for me to pay Mark a visit. Cape Town also happens to be the home of *Kick Off*, virtually the only serious, respected African football magazine. It used to cover South Africa mainly, but since the country had reconnected with the world a few years earlier following the end of apartheid, its interest in football throughout the continent was on the up and its method of working revolutionary by African standards.

South Africa was my second destination in Africa – after Tunisia, where I had been the year before for the Cup of Nations – and my first south of the Sahara. My first encounter with Johannesburg wasn't a bundle of laughs. Luckily I did not have to stay long but this non-city (which I was to have the chance to get to know better a few months later during the Cup of Nations) struck me straight away as a very tough place: a cluster of scattered neighbourhoods, no centre, no soul, no guiding thread. Gilded fortresses and overcrowded townships, long distances and disconnected places, joined only by the sense of unease and fear bound to hit anyone arriving from Europe.

I did not feel safe in Jo'burg, not one bit. I settled down in a house between Yeoville and Berea, the former a neighbourhood full of young people and clubs and bars that rotates round Rockey Street, the latter a home, at that time, to immigrants from Zaire and regarded as dangerous and inhospitable. I decided to take a look around in daylight. I was an attraction, to be stared at, weighed up, assessed in micro-economic terms: 'How much can we make out of the white sucker?' Not a lot, because I soon cut short my impromptu tour and, in any case, I hadn't a penny in my pocket. They tell me that in Yeoville today, the soundtrack of the clubs on Rockey Street is often punctuated by the sound of gunfire. At the time, aside from getting paranoid about using my credit card, I had a favourable impression of the place.

I soon moved on from Johannesburg to Cape Town: the ocean, palm trees, beaches, a much nicer place to live. Yes, the beaches are beautiful, the wine is good and Table Mountain is breathtaking but I shut myself up in the *Kick Off* offices with the dauntingly tall (2.06m) and lanky Mark to start work on my collection. We started with the easy countries, such as South Africa, Nigeria and Ivory Coast. We also made decent progress with Angola, Cameroon and even Sierra Leone. Then the problems started. The Gabon photos were all mixed up; Mark was not sure who was who. But a bit of creative mixing and matching on my part and, much to my South African colleague's amusement, we had assigned a name to every face and were ready to move on. Not all my matches were correct, much to the subsequent disappointment of the Gabonese players – though only they knew how to put the mixed up photos in order.

I came back from South Africa with two-thirds of the album done, plus contacts and ideas about how to find the missing third. Panini wanted all the photos ready by the middle of the August but on the second of the month 52 were still missing: all Liberia, all Morocco, the all-time greats and odd players from Algeria, Cameroon, Egypt, Ghana, Mozambique and Zaire, plus the Tunisian team photo and the shots of the South African cities. Panic! It was like going back to the time when I needed Graziano Bini (Inter), Loris Boni (Sampdoria) and Giampiero Marini (Varese) to complete my 74-75 collection, all really rare, practically unfindable – at least in Rome's Balduina neighbourhood where I used to buy my packets. By August 26 I was still missing 30 cards: then an envelope arrived from Senegal with the photos of Liberia who, certain to qualify for their first African Cup of Nations, had played and lost 3-0 in Dakar on July 30. I celebrated its arrival like the return of the prodigal son. The celebrations did not last for long: the photos were there but the

Senegalese photographer knew none of George Weah's mates, so the same thing happened as for Gabon – it was up to me to match the names with the faces. This time it was even more complicated – it was not a matter of three or four doubts. Apart from the man himself, Weah, and his cousin James Debbah, I couldn't recognise any of the team.

In the meantime, I'd found the missing Algerian and the two Cameroonians, so two more teams were completed. On September 11, 15 cards were still missing. I had received eight Moroccans from a colleague at *Guerin Sportivo*, but not the team line-up. I was also OK for the three Egyptians (thanks to my next door neighbour, Al-Ahram's Rome correspondent Mostafa Abdallah) and the city pics had arrived courtesy of the South African tourist board in Rome. But some problems seemed insurmountable. So I set off north, to give the *Guerin Sportivo* archives in Bologna a shot. There I picked up the nine all-time greats and the Moroccan and Tunisian team photos.

I then headed due north to Milanello, the AC Milan training camp, where I had an appointment with George Weah, the only man in Italy, maybe in the whole world, who could put a name to the photographs of his team-mates that had come in from Dakar. After a training session and a massage, George sat down with me on the steps that led up into the dressing room. King George didn't turn a hair. He was unflappable, keen to help and amused by the job of matching names and faces. He always looked certain, even when he wasn't. We shook hands and promised to meet in South Africa, then I took the train to Rome. The meeting had given me a new lease of life. Now that I'd solved the Liberian problem, there were only four cards to go.

Panini found they had the three missing Zaire players in their archives, though they had to retouch the jerseys (the trio played in Europe and had already appeared in albums for the French or Belgian leagues). All I was lacking now was a player from Mozambique. Anyone would do. I asked Antonio Pereira, a colleague on the Portuguese sports daily *A Bola*, for help. He reckoned that the photo had left Maputo days, if not weeks, earlier. This was not a relief, it was an extra worry. In Cape Town I had found only 14 Mozambique players. In an official African Cup of Nations qualifying match covered by the *Kick Off* photographer, the manager hadn't been able to find other available players. Some of those called up took the field, others had turned up with injuries.

One day on my desk at the Student Tourist Centre in Rome, where I had worked in lieu of military service and where I still worked part-time in the press office, I found a white envelope from Maputo waiting for me among the mail. The album was complete. I opened the envelope frantically and pulled out a black-and-white photograph that looked as if it had come straight out of a 1950s laboratory, a portrait worthy of the Malian Malick Sidibe, one of the best known African photographers. The face of Matias Bebé looked as if it was made of wax, an 'ancient' face, a face I have never forgotten. Bebé was a run-of-the-mill defender who was not even called up for the Cup of Nations, but that hardly mattered. It was the last card: Beltrami would be happy and he would have a bit of colour added at the photo retouch up. The end result would be priceless.

Six months later. The Holiday Inn on the seafront in Durban, South Africa. I'm staying in the same hotel as Liberia, who are playing in the African Cup of Nations. The players get together in the foyer. At the centre of a huge sofa sits Weah, King George, the rest on either side of him apart from the youngest who remain standing to the rear. It is like a group portrait of a patriarchal society. I approach with the album in my hand. George says hello and hurriedly asks what has happened to the work he did for me. 'Here it is,' I reply and hand him the Panini collection. With great ceremony he goes to the Liberia pages, grumbling because his Lone Star team doesn't open the section and to hell with alphabetical order.

He looks for his photo and finds it. The others do the same. Some complain because they are not there, even though they have been picked. I try to explain but then a soft little voice manages to make itself heard. 'That's not me!' Panic and confusion all round. George turns to me with a questioning, vaguely accusatory look. 'That's not me!' Another voice repeats the same words. Then a third says he is in the album but with someone else's name. Everyone is baffled. George stares at me like a prosecutor stares at the most dastardly criminal. 'What have you gone and done?' he asks me. 'Who put the names to the photos?' I reply, defensively but firmly. He mulls it over. What a great actor: he pauses, they all look at him, and he eventually says: 'Me!' They all burst out laughing and start joshing and slapping the boss on the back. George defends himself as best he can. One guy is too young, he says, another looks like someone else, another still had only played in one game... and then there was the quality of the photos, very poor, dim light, bad exposure – you name it. The next day Liberia make their debut in the Cup and beat Gabon 2-1. I snatch the opportunity to put the right names to the right faces in my first finished album.

I continued to work with Panini for another five years, during which I produced nine collections: an African All Stars, another African Cup of Nations, two Moroccan league championships, two Tunisian and one Egyptian, plus a couple of Turkish championships on the side. I also researched the photos of the African teams for the 1998 World Cup. I recall lots of hitches and hold-ups, some collections completed and never published, others never finished due to copyright problems and long, drawn-out negotiations with Tunisian and Moroccan photographers.

I learned to say *baksheesh*, the Arabic word for kickback. It was as precious as gold for me, vital in all the negotiations I was involved in. I learned not to trust 'yeses' said to please and envelopes supposedly in the post for months. The word helped me to get to know the Maghreb and to develop a not overly favourable impression of the place. I made a lot of African photographers happy by buying their pictures and paying through the nose for them. I travelled and I made others travel: strangers, acquaintances and great friends like Andrea Giulio Sesti, a photo-reporter I sent all over the continent to take classic head-and-shoulders shots for Panini. Every journey was an adventure, partly thanks to him, partly due to curious external circumstances.

We needed photos of Nigeria, and the Super Eagles were playing in Guinea in a qualifying match for the World Cup in France. That game, incidentally, marked Nwankwo Kanu's return after a year out following a delicate heart operation but I was interested in Kanu only up to a point. The plunder was the whole team, 20 or so Nigerians to pass on to Modena. Sesti set off for Conakry full of enthusiasm. He was overwhelmed by the place, despite everything. Andrea came back with poetic, realistic black-and-white shots that brilliantly captured the poverty of the city and the country. He also came back with the portraits of the Nigerians: less poetic but very realistic.

Arriving outside the ground at Conakry early on match day, Sesti was impressed by the big crowds. In Africa you can be late in many other situations but you always go to a football match hours before the kick-off. After wandering around a bit, he started to take photographs and thought the long, orderly queues made a good subject. Suddenly the crowd began to disperse as two truckloads of soldiers backed up by an armoured car appeared behind Andrea. He turned round and found himself surrounded. He did not know why he was the object of the Guinean soldiers' attention but he kept his cool. The soldiers flocked round him and roughly beckoned him to get into the armoured car. He demanded explanations but the soldiers did not answer. The atmosphere was getting overheated. Sesti was eventually manhandled into the car, which set off for who knows where.

Before sending him to Conakry, I had spelt out things to Andrea, who I knew had a knack of ending up in tight squeezes. I had told him, in the event of trouble, to look up Monsieur Altafinì (same spelling as the former Brazilian footballer, but with an accent on the final 'i'). In the armoured car, the rough stuff made Andrea's memory go blank. He tried to remember the name of his possible saviour and 20 years of the Brazil national team flashed through his mind, from Rivelino to Socrates. The soldiers were not relenting and he had to find the right password. 'Altafinì!' he shouted all of a sudden.

The car came to a halt as if Andrea himself had stepped on the brake. The word had an almost magical effect. 'Let me talk to him, he's waiting for me.' Andrea was bluffing but it worked. The car made a U-turn and drove back to the stadium. Andrea was ordered to get out without his cameras, which the soldiers hung on to, and taken to Monsieur Altafinì. After much discussion, the boss of the Guinean football federation made a gesture with his hand. Sesti was free again and got his cameras back. But he also received a strict order: 'Never try to photograph the crowd again!' Why? We will never know.

Back from Conakry, Andrea set off for Morocco. After what he had been through in Guinea, he thought it was going to be a doddle. I had warned that the Moroccan federation might be unhelpful and told him to keep a low profile. Morocco were training near Rabat and photographers were allowed to shoot during sessions but as soon as Sesti set foot in the training ground, which was owned by the armed forces, he was stopped. Andrea's rebellious, far-left upbringing had often led him to clash with guards and soldiers of every rank and status, but I was hoping that outside Italy things might work differently. I was wrong. Andrea did not even have time to get his camera out. 'You work for Panini, but this product has already been sold,' they told him in French. How they managed to catch up with him remains a mystery, especially since he was not exactly an elegant dresser and ought to have been able to disappear into the crowd in Rabat. Yet they were right: he was there for Panini and, unbeknown to us, the Moroccan federation had sold the picture rights to someone else.

Trouble brings out the best in Andrea and the next day he turned up at the stadium in Rabat for the national team's match. He didn't want to come home empty-handed and his tactics were clever. He walked into the ground at the very last minute, made a dash for the teams, already lined up for the national anthems, and started taking photographs like a madman. Once more his presence did not go unnoticed; as soon as he got into position, two security officers stepped in and started jostling to prevent him taking any shots. As they tried to drag him away, Andrea started arguing in his Italian-French hybrid. The ensuing scuffle disrupted the playing of the Moroccan national anthem but, before the band had struck the last notes, Sesti had already been ejected from the stadium. Panini had to buy the photos of the *Lions d'Atlas* elsewhere.

Yes, I had learned as a child that it was never easy to complete an album.

5. When the Lions became Indomitable

I t was editor Italo Cucci's brainchild, funded by the Bologna-based sports weekly *Guerin Sportivo* (which no longer has the cash to invest in such ideas). 'Cameroon will be playing Italy in the World Cup. Go and see them against Congo in the quarter-final of the African Cup of Nations and tell us all about the country,' Cucci told me. It involved taking Air Afrique, *l'aerobus* as they call it, from Burkina to Cameroon, via Togo and Nigeria. Relatively speaking it is not a great distance but to make the run profitable a couple of extra stops had been added. The only positive note about this aerial marathon was the duty-free shop in the small airport of Lomé, the capital of Togo. Five hours is a long time for a stopover, but the record shop was attractive and well stocked. I arrived in Douala overloaded with CDs, all bought at bargain prices.

Cameroon v DR Congo was to be played in Bobo Dioulasso, the second city of Burkina Faso, chosen to host matches at the 1998 African Cup of Nations. But I went to see the game in Cameroon itself, on TV in a bar in the port city of Douala, the commercial capital. Despite all its problems, Burkina Faso loves to show itself off as a naive, head-in-the-clouds, poetic, highly positive kind of Africa. Cameroon, however, is a country of scars, of an Africa marked by colonisation. In Ouaga hope exists, even if reasons for it are few and far between. In Douala it is pure desperation: violence and poverty that punches you in the face, a much less amiable vision of life – but there is also plenty of money for the lucky few. Not to mention a desire to exploit even the tiniest opportunity to procure things, anything, by fair means or foul. In Douala they learn to play the game seriously, the aim being to get to Europe to make real money. Or even phoney money, by which I mean the money Cameroonians earn in the ridiculous leagues in which they sometimes play. Or phoney like the ages of certain African footballers. Cameroon has about 500 emigrant footballers scattered round the world, from Barcelona in La Liga to the Indonesian second division. Burkina Faso has only 30 or so expatriates, almost all in the minor divisions in France, Belgium and Germany. The difference is not only one of talent but also of determination, on the field and off.

They had tried to prepare me for the culture shock at Douala airport. In Ouaga, when I was following the African Cup of Nations there, even the Cameroon players would break into laughter when I told them where I planned to go and what I intended to do. 'Keep your eyes peeled at all times,' was the most benevolent piece of advice they had to give me. I had taken the precaution of asking the hotel in Douala to send a car to collect me at the airport. I was unaware that to reach the vehicle, I would have to run the gauntlet of local youths who, at three in the morning, when the plane eventually landed three hours late, had nothing better to do than to harass incoming passengers. Not that anyone lifted a finger to stop the loud, pestering crowd. Once out of the airport, I was welcomed by a wall of humidity. The dry 45-degree heat of Ouaga was immediately a pleasant memory.

At the hotel they wanted to fob me off with a shocking room. I protested but they told me the hotel was fully booked. I asked them to check my booking. I realised there was building work going on: one part of the hotel had been renovated, the other had not. The price of rooms varied and I reckoned I had paid the price of a new one, but had ended up in an old one in the other wing. They told me they could not find my booking. Furious, I barged round to the other side of the counter. I looked for my booking and found my fax. Chambre 427. It was 4.30am when I went up to my room at last. Oh, and the hotel was half empty.

As soon as I left the hotel the following morning, a man stopped me. He told me he had monitored my passport control procedures at the airport and that irregularities had emerged – my visa was invalid and I would have to cough up. I had not slept much and I was half-dazed by the new city but luckily I had no money on me. The man asked for my documents and threatened to take me to the police. I managed to shake him off but he came back again in the afternoon. I gave him the amount he was demanding – not very much – but I had the nasty feeling I had been swindled. The same thing was to happen to me again in Ghana and

Nigeria but, fortified by the first experience, I suggested we take a trip to the nearest police station and the impromptu customs officers both disappeared.

Not that my troubles were over in Douala. On my second day, I visited the football school set up by the local beer king, Gilbert Kadhji, and run by a group of French people, some 20 kilometres out of town. I set off with my Cameroonian guide, who was also a well known sports reporter, plus the French academy coach in the latter's jeep. At the first checkpoint we were stopped. I had forgotten my passport and the policeman asked for $300 to let me through. The Frenchman, who was used to travelling along the road three times a day, lost his temper. He entered into a long, tense negotiation on my behalf, and 20 minutes later we set off again after paying 15,000 *céfas*, roughly £15. For the local police, it was a stroke of good luck, and in their sentry box the passage of the mug tourist was cause for celebration. 'If we'd had more time we could have bargained down to 10,000,' said the Frenchman to cheer me up. At the next road block the coach did not stop at the signal and nor did he stop on the way back, saluting the soldier who had stopped us a few hours earlier with a glorious V-sign. Drunk with their success in the morning, these money grabbers were keen to repeat the trick.

The Omnisport Stadium was a stark block of grey cement in the middle of a cluster of rickety low huts where I saw two league matches (pitches were few and far between, so they exploited incessantly the only ones fit for play until they turned into quagmires). It only took a couple of minutes for hands to get into my backpack in an attempt to steal my camera. I managed to fend them off but it was a nuisance all along. As it was when I walked the 500 metres from my hotel to the nearest internet point. After the first two times, when I had passively resisted all sorts of demands, especially for money, for the whole of the 20 minutes it took to get there, I decided to go in one of the taxi-scooters that whizz around the city all day long.

My five days in Douala were breathless but they did leave me with a few good memories. I got to visit three football schools: one rich, the place I mentioned above, immersed in dense tropical greenery and enhanced by facilities unthinkable for Africa, one average, and one poor. This latter place had a prophetic name, Future Soccer: it consisted of very basic, broken down classrooms, with crumbling walls in which the reinforced concrete core was visible through the bricks, and a makeshift pitch, slippery and very hard, yellow sand on cement, in the internal courtyard. The classroom windows, glassless and frameless, ran all round the pitch and the kids used them as terraces. The official pitch was in a clearing down by the harbour; it was surrounded by huge tree trunks and the goals had limp wires instead of crossbars. The surface was sandy – not too deep but hard to control the ball on.

The only common denominator of the three schools was the joy in playing football and the desire to reach the top. The kids were very strong. They played barefoot or in worn-out shoes or boots, with scuffed balls on uneven surfaces. They played in the schoolyard in ragged shirts in the neighbourhood of Bonaprison and on the regular well kept field of the French-run beer king's academy. Some ran in orderly fashion behind the Frenchman guiding them, others ran in disorderly fashion after the ball, shooting for the goal that would take them closer to Europe. Imagine the large eyes of the kids in front of the camera lens of this white journalist from the country of Serie A, my very presence a sign in itself that something was starting to happen in Douala. The school of the rich produced Samuel Eto'o, taken from Douala to the Real Madrid academy at the age of 15. The school of the poor hadn't produced anyone at that stage, but they had only just begun.

Another pleasant memory takes me back to the suffocating living greenery, continuously growing, of the forest around Mount Cameroon, which stands at an altitude of more than 4,000 metres, 70 kilometres from Douala. It is the Everest of west Africa, a spectacular mountain and a lazy but still active volcano. It was here that Jean Manga Onguene, the Cameroon coach, brought his team before the African Cup of Nations in Burkina Faso, to perform a rite deemed necessary to ward off bad luck. It did not do much good in view of the endless controversy off the field and the mediocre performances on it that followed. At the end of the tournament the coach was kicked out. Superstition in Africa counts for a lot, but not as much as they say it does.

February 20 was the day of Cameroon v DR Congo. The game was to be played in the afternoon. My contact was busy but he did not want me to go off and see the match somewhere on my own. He wanted me to have an escort, so he sent Jean, a young trainee of his. We took a taxi from the Akwa neighbourhood and made for a district whose name sounded like a premonition: Congo. We were not far out of downtown Douala but it felt like being in a different city: naked men shouting or talking to themselves, children playing at making dams in rivulets that collected dubious-looking liquids. Jean had no clear ideas about where to go, so when we got out of the taxi we started looking for the local sports bar. Then, as a gesture of kindness, Jean decided we could see the match at the house of a friend of his with other youths. Tipped off maybe by his more experienced colleague, he wanted to keep me away from the bars at all costs. I entered his friend's house and they offered me a beer. They were very kind but there was no atmosphere. There were only a few of us, plus the rats that scuttled across the floor. I insisted that we continue to look for the right place. I realised that Jean had an idea but he was hesitant to suggest it.

When I eventually managed to get it out of him, we bade our farewells without causing a diplomatic incident and soon after we were in a busy square. On the far side I glimpsed the entrance to a bar: a sort of long, narrow tunnel at the end of which a television set was positioned high up beside the counter. The place was called White House and for any inattentive punters who did not understand the reference, the name was repeated in French, *Maison Blanche*. Not that there was anything presidential about it. To the left you could only just walk in the narrow confined space left by the tables stacked against the wall to the right. The walls were covered with white tiles.

Even though we were not in the notorious port area, there were some shady characters knocking around. Luckily there was the match to watch and the white man, me, managed to pass almost unnoticed. I had thought about taking a few photographs but to keep a low profile I gave Jean the camera. At the third shot, there was almost a riot. Photos obviously were not going to be tolerated so the camera went back to the bottom of my rucksack. We took up a position half way down the tunnel. We ordered bottles of beer and I sat down, with Jean standing behind me to guard me from the rear. I was happy – I couldn't wait to see the match – he less so. The picture was in black and white with a reddish horizontal stripe at the top of the screen and a blueish one at the bottom. It was hard to watch but you got used to it. It reminded me of when as a kid in Rome I used to go up to the Madonnina statue on the Monte Mario, a hill to the north-east of the Vatican. There, from a height and at a distance of about 300

metres, you could see the matches at the Stadio Olimpico. If someone
scored, you realised it was a goal and could celebrate accordingly.

The problem was that after half an hour, it was Congo that scored.
Cameroon were playing terribly and the aficionados in the bar in Douala
were not taking it at all well. But they hadn't given up all hope of an
equaliser. Finally, it happened. In the very last minutes of the game,
Cameroon managed to draw level. The bar exploded. Everybody hugged
one another, some jumped on the tables, bottles fell to the floor and
broke. The celebrations involved everyone, including me. I almost ended
up under one of the formica tables but out of the corner of my eye I caught
a blurred image of the linesman with his flag up. Offside! I got to my feet
and couldn't resist doing my duty as a journalist. 'The goal's been disal-
lowed!' I informed punters. Nobody was looking the screen any more:
the joy was too great to watch the faded images. I waved my arms and
shouted and eventually managed to get the message across.

Suddenly, the Cameroon fans saw me as the embodiment of the
linesman in Bobo Dioulasso. The fucking linesman who had just disal-
lowed a perfectly good goal by the Indomitable Lions. They were still
shouting but this time they were shouting at me. More bottles were
smashed but somehow calm eventually prevailed. The disappointment
was tangible, however. At the end of the match the atmosphere was not
good. My man Jean shoved me out of the place in a hurry. We came
out into the square where the traffic was heavy. A couple rode past on
a scooter and the girl, sitting on the rear seat, thumped me in the back.
Just like that, just for the hell of it. Jean feared the worst and manhandled
me into a taxi. It was best if we changed air sharpish.

In Cameroon football is an affair of state. Not because it is the national
sport or because all politicians also happen to be fans and managers,
but because it is an excellent way of making it big, politically and
economically. In Cameroon money circulates only at the highest level.
The country as a whole is poor and cities like Douala and Yaoundé are
overcrowded with thousands living in abject squalor. Whole neighbourhoods are without sewers and the rain that does not fall for four
months comes all at once. Then the streets become putrid quicksand.
Money is important here more than anywhere else. And football earns
easy money, just as drugs do. This, in part, explains why the Indomitable
Lions' participations in the World Cup and the African Cup of Nations

have always been accompanied by arguments. In 1982 two Italian investigative journalists claimed the *Azzurri* had paid the Cameroonians substantial backhanders to allow the Italians to get the draw they needed to qualify in the final group game. In Italy the rumour did not go down very well but in Cameroon they confirmed it as fact.

In 1990 the man who was supposed to distribute the bonuses for the Lions' fantastic World Cup ran away with the money, leaving the players empty-handed. In 1994, remembering the previous experience, the Indomitable Lions virtually refused to play, putting up memorably poor shows (they conceded six goals to Russia in their final match). Their only concern was to share out the bonuses properly. The same story was repeated at the African Cup of Nations in 1998. Training sessions during the first week were replaced by bickering over the money due for qualifying for France 98 and the expenses for the Burkina tournament. The upshot was that the team played without a game plan, without cohesion, without spirit – and were promptly knocked out in the quarter-finals by the Democratic Republic of Congo.

In 1990 President Paul Biya ordered the arrest of his most dangerous opponent, Yondo Black, who was gaining support every day. Amid growing general protest, lawyers went on strike and people demonstrated in the streets, but it was only in August, after victories in the World Cup in Italy had drawn the attention of half the world to the country, that Biya decided to release his rival.

At the 1998 African Cup of Nations, three people used to speak at the press conferences after the Cameroon matches: the manager Manga Onguene, one of the players and the Minister of Sport and Youth, Joseph Owona. It was the minister, naturally enough, who fielded questions first. Never mind teamsheets, in Cameroon they get straight to the point. The papers attacked the minister, accusing him of wasting public money for his journey to Burkina Faso – a delegation of 62 people, players included, did seem a trifle excessive. But that is the way things are done in Cameroon. The World Cup takes place every four years and it is an irresistible money-making machine. Everyone wants a stake and the battles that break out are veritable battles for survival. A World Cup can change people's lives in Cameroon.

If you want to understand how things happen in Cameroon, look at how the national team is managed, or see what happened in Nsam, the day of the tragedy that cost the lives of 200 people. On February 14, a train carrying petrol derailed in Nsam, a populous neighbourhood of Yaoundé, and petrol started to rain out of the trucks. Instead of being frightened, the people took this as a sign from God. Taxi drivers and motorists attacked the train and bottled the petrol, going backwards and forward to fill their tanks. Then, suddenly, tragedy struck. Investigations have still to clarify the details, but it is known that a discarded cigarette butt set thousands of litres of petrol on fire. All hell let loose – for a free fill-up.
Guerin Sportivo, March 11, 1998

6. I played against Cameroon

'**U**p with oral tradition, down with historical memory.' This is the slogan African football seems to be based on. But when I began to delve deeper, I realised it was a crude way of viewing things. We often speak – wrongly – about Africa as a single entity, turning the continent into one enormous country, but in this case the generalisation works perfectly. From north to south, the style of sports reporting, starting with the match statistics, follows the same track. But the track comes to a dead end. There is nothing to go on. When I decided to gather the statistics for all the African Cup of Nations matches played between 1957, the first year the tournament was held, and 2000 – something that had never been done before – I discovered there were no records of the team line-ups for ten matches between 1963 and 1968. Remember that the Cup of Nations is the backbone of African football, the history of the game on the continent.

After learning the ropes with the first Panini Africa album, I decided to throw myself into an enterprise that I have no qualms about describing as inhuman. Without the financial backing of the Modena company, I contacted a small Tuscan publisher and started collecting data. In January 1999, my first African football annual came out. It included fact sheets of matches played by national teams, lists of players called up for internationals and potted biographies of African players in Europe complete with statistics of matches played, goals scored and so on. It was tough work, admittedly, but it was also an act of love, especially since it was targeted at an audience that could be euphemistically described as 'niche'. In Africa itself, this sort of publication is of very little interest. Let's say that the absence of such information had never been noticed and its appearance met with a very cool reception.

I continued with the annual for four years and in the second I formed a publishing company of my own: Filippo Maria Ricci Editore. I used to print 2,000 copies and, with a considerable amount of effort, managed to sell just over 1,500 to the few bookshops that showed interest (eight in the whole world) and to individual fans and enthusiasts. This allowed me to build up a reputation as a guru of statistics applied to African football – talk about specialisation! – and to meet a lot of wild and wonderful characters: from the doorman at the Ministry of Transport in Rome, who became a regular client, to the translator at the Court of Luxembourg, a book collector with a shop in his house.

When I moved to London, I was forced to work daily on more lucrative projects to keep up with the cost of living. I had to suspend the project and relax my African football obsession, though I have not yet surrendered to the idea of giving it up for good. FMRE also published a history of Nigerian football written by a university professor who emigrated to America and the volume, mentioned earlier, on the African Cup of Nations. Then it closed down, after earning itself, with merit but without profit, a place in the history of football publishing with a total of five volumes all devoted to the game in Africa.

Five years on, I still receive queries and requests and letters of encouragement from all over the world. I only have a few disciples, though: the work involved is onerous to say the least and so far no one has bothered to follow my example. True, a Norwegian enthusiast has published a list of African professionals playing in Europe but he has neglected the part about national-team call-ups. Today the African football tradition is all in the hands of a single person, Mark Gleeson, the giant South African journalist who, after being granted free access to the FIFA archives in Zurich, was then sent to the CAF headquarters in Cairo to bring order to an archive that was as untidy as a teenager's bedroom, thus turning chaos into an art form. Today Mark collects, photocopies and archives, keeping himself up to date on the almost 50 African national teams and registering debuts and caps, all from his home in Cape Town.

The question of appearances in national teams is the most complex of all. Statistics that are considered important, hence virtually taken for granted, in Europe do not even exist in Africa. Since Gleeson entered the scene with post-apartheid South Africa in the early 1990s, at least the major national-team records have been properly classified but the data is not in the public domain, so a certain amount of groping in the dark is still called for. For the smaller countries, definite facts and figures are impossible to come by. At one point in his long career – which, incidentally, has not yet finished – the Egyptian Hossam Hassan broke the world record for the highest number of national-team appearances. The Egyptian federation sent the full list to FIFA but in Zurich they were unsure. They passed it on to Gleeson. The South African erased a few questionable matches from the list and reduced the total number of appearances, but the record stayed (though it has since been beaten by Saudi Arabia's Mohamed Al-Deayea). Not that anyone could swear to its credibility. Lower down the ladder, the view gets even mistier, with false information confusing things further. This is a pity because there are very few books about African football and its countless stories. The years go by and as the repositories of recollections grow old, so historical memory is lost.

In 1998, the Panini albums and my odd job as an 'African football expert' allowed me to record another curious chapter in the story. One late afternoon towards the end of April, I received a phone call from a certain Carlo Bianconi, a total stranger who told me he owned a nice hotel in Norcia, in the Umbria region of central Italy, complete with an immaculate football pitch. 'Bring me an African national side to train here before the World Cup!' he demanded. 'Salvatore Lo Presti at the *Gazzetta dello Sport* told me you're the only person capable of pulling off the miracle.'

At least he was honest enough to use the right word, 'miracle'. Bianconi knew it was a tough mission but he also knew that African national teams do not stand out for their ability to plan ahead. So he was trying his luck. Umbria had been hit by an earthquake just months earlier and the Regional Authority had made funds available to revive the area. The World Cup was due to begin in France in a matter of months and three of the African teams that had qualified had just changed their managers. In January Nigeria had signed up Bora Milutinovic and on April 11 Cameroon had given the job to Claude Le Roy, a sign that the life of the national team manager in Africa is harder and more precarious than anywhere else – but also a glimmer of hope for me in terms of pre-World Cup disorganisation.

I called Le Roy, the blond French coach who had built, lost, then rebuilt a reputation for himself in Africa, doing a particularly good job in Cameroon and Senegal. He had just been called back to the helm of the Indomitable Lions. I offered him a deal: a week's residence free, all expenses paid. Nice place, healthy air, good food, excellent facilities, total peace and quiet. All the federation had to pay for was the air fares. The only drawback was that Italy were in the same group at the World Cup. Some players and officials were unhappy about that. They were frightened of being spied on, as if they had God-knows-what special moves or secrets to hide. In my first-generation VW Golf I went down to pick up Le Roy at Rome's airport, Fiumicino, and drove him to Norcia. The moustachioed Frenchman hated the journey, which was longer than he had imagined. He also had a bad back and found the car uncomfortable. That night the journeying continued as we had to go to Parma to see Italy play Paraguay in friendly, the highlight of which turned out to be an overhead kick scored by Checco Moriero. We went there in Bianconi's son's Mercedes, a blessing for the bad back of Le Roy, French by birth but African by adoption.

He liked what he saw in Norcia and Cameroon liked the idea of a free stay there. The Indomitable Lions thus decided to ignore their fear of industrial espionage and were glad to accept the invitation to Umbria. They had me fearing the worst when they were a week late in arriving but that was just a minor hiccup.

It was thus that I ended up spending five days in Norcia with Cameroon, trying to assist the players, coaches and officials as much as possible. It was a great experience, though it was spoilt slightly when Marc-Vivien Foé broke a leg in training. That was a body blow for the Lions as a team and for Foé himself, who was about to sign for Manchester United. The highlights of the experience were: the long chats with the players; the doctor who came from Fiumicino to Norcia by taxi, a fare of over 400,000 lire (more than £100); the visit of comedienne Luciana Litizzetto on behalf of the Italian TV comedy team Gialappa's Band; and the young Lauren, who would eventually play for Arsenal and Portsmouth and who had just been picked for the national team but was always on his own since he had grown up in Spain and spoke only Spanish – no French and no African language. Then there was the match itself. I reported it in the *Guerin Sportivo* under the headline **I swear, I played against Cameroon**.

For a journalist who writes only about African football, the idea of playing against the Indomitable Lions was a dream. But it came true last Sunday afternoon at the Stadio Comunale in Norcia. Claude Le Roy's Cameroon, the second opponents of the *Azzurri* in the World Cup, took the field against Walter Boccolini's Norcia and, for over half an hour, I got the chance to stick to the heels of Patrick Mboma and his team-mates. I behaved a bit like the spoilt kid in the park, walking into the dressing rooms and saying 'The ball's mine, so I've got to play'. I had organised the match and Norcia played in the *seconda categoria*, the same non-league championship as Tottenham 90, my team in Rome. Manager Boccolini readily agreed and handed me a shirt. I thus turned from being the photographer-narrator of the feats of the Indomitable Lions into a (technically) improbable opponent.

I watched them play from the bench, and at half-time started to warm up. I was ready and in the tenth minute of the second half the manager sent me on. It was 10-0 to them and I played right-back. In my zone were striker Mboma and two young hopefuls, Meyong Ze, an attacking midfield player, and Saidou, a left-back [nine years on, both still play in the national team]. Mboma was so fast I could not even grab his jersey: on the dirt pitches on the Via Cassia, in Rome, I had never seen such strength combined with such speed. I cleared the ball a couple of times, then at a corner I played it crafty, getting a team mate to mark the giant while I stood on the goal-line.

Regular as clockwork, the cross came over for Mboma, who headed down powerfully towards the corner of the net, where I was standing and, with my arm (glued to my body), managed to avoid goal number 11. The mark of the diamonds on the ball was to stay on my skin for a week – and that was only a header! In the next attack, a long ball was played to Mboma down the wing. I anticipated him and I was sure I was going to intercept the ball. In the space of a second, I looked around and they weren't there any more. Neither Mboma nor the ball, both now a long way off. You don't see the difference on television and you're tempted to think 'I could have scored that'. But it is all a question of pace, speed of movement and thought and strength of shooting. Before you can control the ball, there is someone snapping away at your heels. Non-stop pressing. My team-mates were moaning, and when they realised I knew our opponents, they asked me to talk to them: 'Let us try to make the first pass before you press!' I begged. I called them by name, I asked them to give us a breather, but it was useless. The Lions were keyed up; each was fighting for a first-team place and they allowed us no respite. If one failed to press, there was another ready to tell him off.

I personally managed to make a couple of passes and an amateurish hoof out of the penalty area, much to the crowd's delight. But I also got nutmegged by Meyong Ze – I still don't know how he got the ball through my legs – and tried in vain to make a couple of sliding tackles: I felt like Andreas Brehme but by the time I was scraping across the grass, my opponent had long since flashed by with ball, leaving me no time even to trip him or knock him off balance. I did have the satisfaction of being chased by Mboma, who grabbed my shirt as I was trying to play him offside. In one rare attack we actually won a penalty. But, hypnotised by the keeper, the talented local No 10 missed it.

The referee blew his whistle. Final score: 12-0. As far as I was concerned, it was a success. Just two goals conceded in the 35 minutes I was on the pitch and compliments from our opponents. 'You aren't as bad as I thought you'd be,' were the kind words of Claude Le Roy. I thanked him and left the pitch. An unforgettable experience!

Filippo Ricci, Guerin Sportivo, African football expert

Yes, that's exactly what they wrote under my name: African football expert.

7. The big heart of Africans

H ere's how I reported the tragic death of the Cameroonian inter-national Marc-Vivien Foé in the *Corriere della Sera, Gazzetta dello Sport* and *Guerin Sportivo.*

Breaking news

Marc-Vivien Foé died in Lyon yesterday aged 28. A member of the Cameroon national team, he played in Europe, in France and England, for ten years. He had a powerful physique and a pleasant, shy, touching smile. He slumped to the ground in the centre-circle of the Gerland stadium in the 71st minute of the Cameroon v Colombia Confederations Cup semi-final, which his compatriots went on to win 1-0. He fell unconscious, in the stadium where he had played for two seasons from 2000, winning the French League Cup in 2001 and the French Championship the year after. After 45 minutes of fruitless attempts to save him, doctors declared him dead. Mouth-to-mouth resuscitation and cardiac massages were attempted but to no avail. 'The causes of death are still not entirely clear,' announced the FIFA doctor Alfred Mueller. 'We will have to wait for the results of the autopsy.'

Some blamed the heat, but Foé grew up in temperatures much higher than the 30 degrees Celsius in Lyon yesterday; some blamed the number of matches he had played back to back, but the midfielder had been on the pitch for only 154 of the 270 minutes Cameroon played in the tournament. What seems certain is that Foé's heart stopped. Routine football injuries apart, the Cameroon midfielder had never suffered from health problems. Foé had ten seasons behind him, playing in Europe for Lens, West Ham, Lyon and Manchester

City, so it seems incredible that no one ever noticed anything amiss. One thinks back to Nwankwo Kanu, the Nigerian who moved from Ajax to Inter, where he was saved by the club's medical staff and the affection of Massimo Moratti.

Fate thus seems to have put an end to the life of a quiet young man, reserved but always ready to help, loved by his team mates in Europe and respected like an old village chief by his fellow countrymen in Cameroon – especially now that with the arrival of a clutch of young Indomitable Lions, he had become one of the leaders of the group. FIFA decided to go ahead with the second semi-final of the tournament between France and Turkey, and the sadness of the France players is the most living testimony to the memory left by Foé. The faces of Henry, Gallas, Coupet and the others were lined with tears, for a friend more than for a team-mate or an opponent.

Foé was born in Yaoundé, the capital of Cameroon, on May 1, 1975, and his name began to circulate in Europe in 1993. After losing the African Under-20 Cup final against Ghana in Mauritius, Cameroon set out for Australia, where they came third in their first-round group in the world equivalent. An Italian agent who was present was impressed by the midfielder from Canon of Yaoundé and recommended him to Fiorentina. But the directors of the Florence club were not taken with the tall, slightly awkward youth, and in 1994 Foé ended up at Lens in France, where he stayed until 1999. In the meantime, he was a member of the Indomitable Lions' disastrous expedition to the 1994 World Cup in the USA, and played in the African Cup of Nations in 1996 and 1998.

That year Foé won the French league with Lens, earning the praise of no less a manager than Sir Alex Ferguson. So this skilful defensive midfield player, intelligent and good with his head, signed for Manchester United and left for pre-World Cup training in Italy. At the camp in Norcia, alas, Foé broke his leg in a tackle with a team-mate – goodbye World Cup, goodbye Manchester. After a wasted season, he eventually did arrive in England but at West Ham. Things did not work out in London, however, and he returned to France, where at first he was a shadow of his former self. Moving to Lyon, he returned to his former level of play. He went on to win a League Cup and League title and also did well in the Champions League. He was decisive in Cameroon's double success in the African Cup of Nations in 2000 and 2002, and last year he at last went to Manchester, not to United but to Kevin Keegan's City on loan. It was to be his last season but it was a superb one: 35 matches played and nine goals scored, many of them decisive and spectacular.

Just yesterday afternoon before Foé took the field in Lyon, his agent Willy McKay had announced that he had received six offers for his client. Manchester City wanted him at all costs but Lyon were haggling about the price. Today all this talk is worthless.

Corriere della Sera, June 27, 2004

The day after

From celebration to tragedy. On Thursday afternoon the streets of Douala and Yaoundé, the two main cities in Cameroon, filled up with people ready for a party. The Indomitable Lions had beaten Colombia to reach the final of the Confederations Cup. Then, suddenly, silence fell. Word spread through the streets, the tragic news had passed from mouth to mouth: '*Foé est mort*'. People cursed and wept, the streets emptied as fast as they had filled up, and the shutters on the bars were lowered. The great funeral wake had begun. In Cameroon commercial radio stations are as popular as they are in Madrid or Rome: lots of football and, this being Africa, lots of music. For the whole day yesterday, the country's stations were inundated with phone calls.

Everyone had something to say, a word or a story in memory of the hero who has died suddenly on a football pitch. The calls alternated with music, the DJs battling it out to find the favourite record of 'Marco', the gentle giant of the Cameroon midfield. In the Mimboman neighbourhood, not far from the Ahmadou Ahidjo Stadium, where Foé had begun playing football ten years earlier, his parents' house has become a place of pilgrimage: relatives, friends, fans, ordinary people. His father is alone in Yaoundé; his wife, Marco's mother, is in Lyon to assist their daughter-in-law who, two months ago, gave birth to the Foé family's third child. The father has hung a photo of his son from the 2000 African Cup of Nations victory on the door of the house and, in the living room, another of Marc-Vivien receiving an award from the president of Cameroon, Paul Biya, after the 2002 victory. The room is open to anyone who wants to come in and offer a word of comfort.

In Europe countless messages of sympathy continue to flow in – a river of fond words. The mayor of Lyon has declared that a stadium will be named after Foé. The president of FIFA, Joseph Blatter, will promote a project to dedicate the Confederations Cup to the late midfielder. Roger Milla, who in his never-ending career still managed to play with Foé in the 1994 World Cup at the age of 42, has announced that 'Cameroon will play in the final against France because that's what Marco would have wanted'. His words triggered controversy, and criticisms of the decision flew in from all quarters, from everyone from former Marseille, AC Milan and Chelsea player Marcel Desailly to Sergio Campana, president of AIC, the Italian professional footballers' association.

Marco really wanted to do well in this tournament. 'Even if it means dying, we've got to get to the final' – according to defender Rigobert Song, those were the words Foé used after the first half of the Cameroon v Colombia match to gee up his team-mates. 'It's incredible, I can't believe this has happened,' added Song. 'Foé was like a brother to me. We grew up together in the streets of Yaoundé, we lived close to each other. We've got to try to get over this terrible moment together and win the tournament for him. Then we'll take him back to Cameroon to bury him.' On Sunday Cameroon will play the final in all-white shirts, on their chests Foé's name and his dates of birth and death. Special shirts for a special team-mate, who died playing football.

Gazzetta dello Sport, June 28, 2004

Looking for a reason why

'Initial analyses have shown nothing abnormal, but we can rule out that Foé died of a heart attack. Toxicological tests will be carried out over the next few days and it will take some time before we have the results.' This is the statement issued by the Lyon public prosecutor, Xavier Richaud, following the death of Marc-Vivien Foé. Foé is dead, but the reason why is still unknown. Watching the scene on television, the doctor of the French national side suggested the possibility of an aneurysm, but the autopsy has ruled this out. One possible hypothesis is that of a congenital illness, something that had evaded detection and which Foé may have carried with him since childhood.

Corriere della Sera, June 28, 2004

Confirmation

An important clue to the cause of the death of the Cameroonian footballer Marc-Vivien Foé has been revealed in England. Yesterday the *News of the World* quoted Harry Redknapp, the manager who signed Foé for West Ham in January 1999, who said the player initially failed the London-based club's medical. Doctors had apparently expressed doubts about the size of the midfielder's heart, deemed too large in proportion to his rib cage. A specialist then gave his approval, however, and Redknapp was able to complete the signing from Lens for £4 million.

Redknapp is reported as saying that it looked as if Foé's extra-large heart might constitute a problem but that a specialist subsequently explained that the condition was absolutely normal and common among African sportsmen. West Ham thus went through with the signing. Redknapp's account has been confirmed by Peter Storrie, MD at West Ham at the time. According to Storrie, the problem revealed by the medical had to do with the size of Marc's heart, but once the club had received the go-ahead from doctors it had no hesitation in signing the player. Before joining West Ham, the midfielder spent four-and-a-half years at Lens, and after his spell in London moved on to Manchester City. Nobody felt it was necessary to stop Foé. If the Cameroonian had come to play in Italy, perhaps things might have gone differently. Faced with cases similar to Foé's, Treviso (Serie B) and Potenza (Interregionale) decided not to sign two young Ivory Coast players, Adama Niambele and Yussouf Kone.

Pending the completion of all the post-mortem tests, light is beginning to be shed on the causes of his death. Yesterday the president of FIFA, Joseph Blatter, categorically ruled out the possibility of drug-related problems.
Corriere della Sera, June 30, 2004

Funerals
Following a massive tribute in the mortuary chapel in Lyon yesterday afternoon, the funeral of Marc-Vivien Foé will be held in the cathedral of St Jean today. The Cameroonian footballer's coffin will then be taken to Paris and thence, accompanied by the full national squad, to Cameroon, where a state funeral will be held on July 12 in the Catholic cathedral of Yaoundé.
Gazzetta dello Sport, July 3, 2004

The letter
I was particularly moved by the death of Marc-Vivien Foé, because I had known him for years, because I am particularly tied to African football and because his death could perhaps have been avoided. For the first time I found myself writing on the spot about a very sad event. I wished to convey my fondness for Marc but I was afraid of sounding pathetic. In 1993 my brother Domenico, who had spent ten years in Zaire before embarking on a career as an agent, returned from the African Under-20 Cup in Mauritius. Gargo and Kuffour's Ghana had beaten Cameroon in the final, and my brother was fixated with the young Lions' best player, Marc-Vivien Foé. Marc's was thus one of the first names to enter my memory, which over the years was to get clogged up with data from Africa.

I came across him again in 1996 at the African Cup of

Nations in South Africa and then, for longer, at the Cup again in Burkina Faso. Foé was born in the north of Cameroon and only moved to Yaoundé later, so he was a bit different from more exuberant team-mates born and bred in Yaoundé or in the rough port city of Douala. He was a reserved, shy young man, but always ready to help and incredibly well mannered. Foé was quietly making headway in the group of the Indomitable Lions. Everything was going well but not, alas, for him. After two days in pre-World Cup training in Norcia, in Italy, he broke a leg in a tackle with a team-mate.

I remember the sadness and desperation on the faces of the other players and the medical staff, emotions that suggested something more than just the loss of a good team-mate. Marc 'the silent' was already a leader of that team, on and off the field, thanks to his passion for music. The atmosphere in the training camp changed. In 2000 I again spent a lot of time with Cameroon, this time in Ghana for the African Cup of Nations, which they won in Lagos, Nigeria. With Song and Mboma, Foé was now one of the oldest members of the group, and in Africa elders are listened to and respected. Foé, with his shy, melancholic smile, won the affection and admiration of anyone who met him.

Oddly enough, in the summer of 2000 I had the pleasure of getting to know the other face of the Foé family. In London on a surveillance mission prior to going to live there, I decided to follow the Inner City World Cup of foreign communities: 32 teams, two days of football. Cameroon did well (though Sierra Leone won) and for the BBC I interviewed their strong central defender, Emmanuel Foé, the younger brother of Marc-Vivien, whom he had accompanied to London after his transfer to West Ham from Lens. Same smile, same kindness, same obliging character. Attempts to find a reason for Marc's sudden death have led me to make discoveries and reflections. What if Foé's transfer to Fiorentina really had gone through? Things might have been different – but destiny decided otherwise.
Guerin Sportivo, July 8, 2004

The African anomaly

Foé was buried in the area of the Okoui neighbourhood in Yaoundé he had chosen for the building of a personal sports complex. It was an old idea of Marc's to donate to his country a modern, efficient sports facility, complete with football pitch, athletics track, Olympic-size swimming pool and tennis courts. On his death, the Cameroon government had pledged to fund the project, which was to cost an estimated $6 million, but months later Foé's father Martin complained he had never received a single franc from the government.

In Italy there has been no shortage of cases of African footballers with serious health problems, but all have been addressed scrupulously and with great professional commitment by the doctors of the clubs involved. From Internazionale and Udinese to Treviso and Potenza, from Serie A to the non-league Interregionale, from north to south, we have seen many examples of African footballers in distress – in chronological order, Nwankwo Kanu, Stephen Appiah, Adama Niambele, Yussouf Kone and Khalilou Fadiga – and of their clubs standing by them.

The most famous case is that of Kanu. The Nigerian striker came to Inter from Ajax for seven billion lire (£2.5 million) in July 1996 with an Olympic gold medal round his neck. It was the first time the Olympic football competition had been won by Nigeria and, more importantly, the first time it had been won by a team from Africa. Kanu was only 20, but in his three years in Holland he had already won the Champions League, the Intercontinental Cup and three league titles. He seemed to be enjoying excellent health. At Inter, however, they noticed immediately that he had a serious heart condition, a valve that failed to function properly.

Kanu was thus sent to Cleveland in the United States for an operation, then monitored, cured and restored to football, free of risk. 'Kanu was born with a deformed aortic valve which had begun to leak and influence cardiac functions,' explained the American heart surgeon John Kramer. Odd that they hadn't noticed anything untoward at Ajax. The treatment Kanu underwent was very costly but also effective. In three years at Inter Kanu played only 12 league games, but after being sold to Arsenal he returned to his old high standards. Previously Kanu had been able to play, but by playing he risked death. Inter stopped him, but that hadn't happened elsewhere. Today the Nigerian, conscious of the great risk he ran, has opened the Kanu Heart Foundation, a charity organisation to help other sportsmen and women.

Ghanaian Stephen Appiah's problem was different altogether. Appiah, who now plays for Fenerbahce in Turkey after ten years or so in Serie A, was brought to Italy by Udinese. In 1999 he moved to Parma but after the Under-20 World Cup in Nigeria and a holiday in Ghana, the doctors noticed that he had contracted a very violent form of Hepatitis B, also known as serum. Despite excruciating pain and a disease that would have floored anyone else, Appiah incredibly went on playing. Yet the problem was extremely serious. The transfer to Parma fell through and the Pozzo family, owners of Udinese, contacted Dr Fagioli at the University of Padua, whose team was at the forefront of research into the disease. The doctor's treatment had yet to be approved in Italy, so Appiah, like Kanu, was forced to go to the US, to Chicago. After a long stay in hospital and an even longer rehabilitation period, he eventually returned to top form.

The Treviso and Potenza cases take us back to heart conditions, both identical to the one that cost Foé his life. Adama Niambele and Yussouf Kone – two kids from Ivory Coast, both good players – arrived in Italy full of hope. 'The Treviso directors grew very fond of Niambele,' recalls Alessandro Zenari, the agent of the two youngsters, 'and, together with their medical staff, they did everything they could to find a solution to the problem. Dr Sarto, the club doctor, came with us when we took Niambele to the Gemelli general hospital in Rome but there was nothing we could do. In Italy tests are stringent and no chances are taken. Niambele, like Kone, was sent home to Ivory Coast. But Dr Sarto told us that in other countries the lad would have got the go-ahead from doctors because the general belief is that a big heart is normal among African athletes.' Which is exactly what the specialist who examined Foé told West Ham. Niambele's career in Italy was cut short but he did not give up – he was desperate to make it. Thanks to a former team-mate, he managed to get to Denmark, where he played with second level Thisted FC in 2006-07.

In Kone's case, too, they diagnosed a problem of cardiac hypertrophy and the subsequent story was the same. He was taken home by the people who had brought him to Italy in the first place, then signed for Raja Casablanca, in Morocco, with whom he lost the African Champions League final in 2002. Kone now plays in Norway with Rosenborg and he played and scored in the 2007-08 Champions League. He has even changed nationality, receiving *Burkinabé* citizenship and playing for the Burkina Faso national team.

Here we come to the other side of the problem. There may be unscrupulous clubs and compliant or imprudent doctors around but it is also true that, for African youngsters, a contract with a European (or Moroccan) club can change their lives, or at least their current circumstances. Prospects outside football are so poor or intangible that it is only too easy to come to the conclusion that it's worth playing even if that means risking your life. Moreover, medical results and verdicts often arrive when you have been playing for a while: a youngster struggles to accept and convince himself that, from one day to the next, he has to abandon something he has done for years.

This is exactly what Khalilou Fadiga said when they told him it would be mad for him to go on playing, that just being hit by the ball could cost him his life. The Senegalese player was due to join Inter from Auxerre in the summer of 2003. But the Italian club's medical staff discovered a dangerous cardiac arrhythmia and blocked the transfer. Fadiga had spent 11 seasons as a professional in Belgium and France and not one of the seven clubs he had played for had stopped him, just as Ajax had not stopped Kanu. Fadiga did not give up and in May 2004 he underwent open-heart surgery.

Following rehabilitation, he began to look around for a new team. After being turned down by several clubs – including Olympique de Marseille, run by his compatriot, friend and former agent Pape Diouf, who blocked the transfer on medical advice after he had decided to sign the player – he was signed by Bolton in the Premier League. In October 2004 he turned out for the reserves and then in the League, 16 months after his last match, Senegal v Lesotho. Ten days later, during the warm-up for a cup match against Tottenham, Fadiga fainted and slumped to the ground. He was rushed to hospital; there were fears for his life and obvious doubts about whether he could continue playing or not.

The same night in Brazil, Serginho of São Caetano died of a heart attack during a match. Two days later, in the Belgian town of Alost, Fadiga had a defibrillator fitted and started hoping again. On December 17 the doctors gave him the thumbs-up to start training again and four days later Fadiga turned out for Bolton against Manchester City in a reserve match. He celebrated his 30th birthday at the end of 2004 and he started 2005 with an away match against Ipswich.

In early December 2004, asked about the Senegalese player's condition, Professor Marcello Chimienti, the Italian doctor who had first diagnosed the arrhythmia in 2003, had been very blunt: 'Fadiga should stop playing football and live a quiet life. In Italy no team would field a player with a defibrillator. It is a gadget that can stop as easily as it works. It is so delicate that during a match, if you're hit by the ball or receive a knock from an opponent or fall on your shoulder, it could stop and that would mean immediate death. Fadiga shouldn't be allowed to play and another operation wouldn't change things a bit.' Fadiga himself holds a different view and continues to go his own way. He played his last game in April 2007 for Coventry City where his career was ended by a tendon injury.

8. Impressions of Nigeria

That Nigeria was a country in a category of its own within Africa became clear to me immediately. I was queuing for my visa at the embassy in Rome's Prati neighbourhood when my attention was caught by a huge poster plastered over most of a booth that cut the waiting room in half. It was a half-length portrait of a man drowning in the cloud of smoke created by the joint he was smoking. The man was Fela Anikulapo Kuti, inventor of Afro-beat and one of the fathers of Nigerian music, a great musician but also a poet, politician, subverter, leader and prophet. Tried 365 times and jailed, beaten up and tortured, in that huge portrait of his, in Rome at least, Fela Kuti was pulling the leg of a government that had never loved him. Nigeria is a country of many contradictions, and the Fela poster in the embassy was shouting the message out to me loud and clear.

Five years earlier, also in Rome, I had a similar experience. I was in the Wazobia restaurant to watch Italy v Nigeria in the last 16 of the 1994 World Cup. The audience was mixed: it ranged from the Communist Euro MP Dacia Valent, who had shifted right politically and was expecting a billionaire's child, to the larger-than-life Roman journalist Luca Giurato, who had come to the restaurant to do a colour piece for RAI television. Both unlikely characters for such an occasion. We were near Rome's Termini station so there were also a hundred or so Nigerians – in Italy for work, some of it legal, some of it less so – a few reporters and a some curious onlookers. All watching an outdated 14-inch TV set which, in the 20th minute, had replaced a larger, more stylish model that had melted in the heat.

My loyalties were divided. I had been supporting African teams since going to Naples to see England against Cameroon four years earlier. The Lions had lost 3-2, after wasting many chances and playing naively but that exciting, unforgettable game had been my rite of passage from

Anglophilia to Africanism. I did not like Arrigo Sacchi's Italy ('Sacchi's glasses are like Stevie Wonder's,' said one Nigerian diner at Wazobia, perfectly seriously. 'That's why Italy are playing badly. The manager's blind!') but they were nonetheless my national team. It was an intense afternoon – smells, colours, heat – and it allowed me to become familiar with some of the *leitmotifs* of football passion in Africa. As far as the fans are concerned, any match is over even before it is played. That afternoon forecasts ranged from 2-0 to 3-1 for the Super Eagles. Celebrations sometimes get underway a good 20 minutes before the final whistle is blown. Never mind superstition, never mind common sense, the Nigerians were beating Italy 1-0 and in the Esquilino area of Rome, and I presume also in Lagos and Ibadan, the party began very early. Boozing, singing, dancing.

When Roberto Baggio scored his first goal, which took the match into extra time, during which he scored again to knock Nigeria out of the Cup, many Wazobia customers were already outside in Via Alfredo Cappellini partying on the pavement. Just after the final whistle, a grumpy character appeared on a balcony on the third floor of the house opposite. He made an gesture and shouted in Roman dialect '*V'avemo rotto er culo!*' (We've whupped your ass!). A verbal brawl ensued in which objects were thrown. Things only calmed down when a squad car arrived from the police station nearby. I learned a few classic Nigerian fans' chants: from 'Over the bar', the funky prayer-cum-chant they sing when opponents have a free-kick on the edge of box, and the old mantra 'All we are saying is give us a goal'. The Nigerians did need another goal, but their prayers went unanswered. Everything was fine just the same. Giving 'mighty Italy' a fright was tantamount to a victory.

Fear and loathing in Lagos, never mind Las Vegas. Hunter S Thompson could easily have adapted his famous novel to Nigeria's leading city, not the administrative capital, which was shifted to Abuja, in the centre of the country, in 1991, but the true heart of the nation. A monster of a city with a population of more than ten million, many of them rich, a multitude also very poor. Beautiful in parts, but also dirty and bad.

Arriving in Lagos is a shock in itself. Take any guidebook, from the swankiest to the no frills *Lonely Planet*, and you will find that the intro-ductions are always pretty much identical. Running the gauntlet of the Murtala Mohammed Airport can be an awful experience. Tolls to pay, psychological torture, all manner of headaches, from passport and health controls to body searches and a detailed baggage check. It is enough to put you off. Then outside, if no one comes to collect you, you are thrown into a pitched battle right away.

Nigeria is the most populous country in Africa. The last census was carried out in 1963, but the estimated population today is 120 to 140 million. Nigeria is like a continent in itself. There are about 250 ethnic groups and over 400 dialects are spoken. Under the country's green-and-white flag live enormous differences in religion, lifestyle, attitude and philosophy. In Lagos they tell you to go to hell before they say hello. They are tough and prickly and full of themselves. But if you overcome the first impact, you discover people who are bright, breezy and on the ball. If you are prepared for this, you get used to it; if you are frightened or react the wrong way, all conversation ends. If you answer back, they laugh and interesting friendships can develop. This is why first impressions may be deceiving in Nigeria. Sometimes circumstance forces you to go on them but if you manage to dig deeper, which may mean moving out of Lagos or making the person you are talking to lower their suspicious guard, you discover a country full of resources.

My personal experience during the Under-20 World Cup in 1999 was exciting: fraught with difficulties, mostly of a practical nature, but packed with positive surprises. The people, as in many other African countries, want to talk and discuss and argue. In Burkina Faso they do so in a very calm, measured way but in Nigeria they get agitated. It happens every time, even when they are talking about things that are a long way off or of minor significance. A mixture of passion, disillusion, forcefulness – especially in Lagos, a city of people who see every sight imaginable every day of their lives.

On my arrival, I received preferential treatment. I was scared stiff, what with all the stories I had heard about the place. I was travelling with Gianni Dini, an anarchist first and a scout for Udinese second. Though he had travelled widely in Africa and loved the continent profoundly, even he did not feel at ease. On the plane, to prepare for the impact, every time he saw a hostess he ordered two whiskies, one for him and one for me – but they always turned into a double for him as I did not want mine and gave it straight back. Landing in Lagos, a surprise was in store for us. We only had to utter the magic word 'FIFA' and we were catapulted into a comfortable lounge on the first floor, where we were cossetted with cool Coca-Cola and biscuits as we waited for customs formalities to be completed. No check, no queue, no demands for money. No nothing. We left and found our suitcases in a car we had not ordered but that was there waiting to take us to the hotel. This is the other face of Nigeria, a Nigeria of uncompromising power, a Nigeria capable of anything.

FIFA had decided to hold the Cup – with teams from 20 important and not so important footballing nations, from England to the United States, Japan to Argentina – in Nigeria on Sepp Blatter's incontestable order. The *presidentissimo* owed Africa a debt for the support he had received in the previous year's elections, and he fought all and sundry to keep his word. FIFA had conducted ten visits to Nigeria before the tournament and reports to Zurich were by no means positive. Anything but. Pressure was exerted to change the host nation: there was no lack of alternatives, after all. But Blatter was determined to keep his promise. At all costs. Nigeria thus underwent an enforced moral crusade for the three-week duration of the event. A press accreditation around your neck guaranteed the same amount of immunity as a representative of a UN peacekeeping force. The order was imperative: keep your hands off anyone down here for the Cup. The situation that ensued was almost surreal. In a flurry of puritanism, hundreds of preventive arrests were made and some people were detained for the three weeks, just enough time to let the FIFA officials come and go.

The day after our arrival in Lagos, we ran into a singular demonstration. Prostitutes were parading half-naked through the streets of the centre to protest against being chased out of all the hotels in town, as a result of a late and clumsy attempt to straighten out moral principles, again for the statutory three weeks. 'How come,' the women protested, 'we were always in the hotels and now all of a sudden you chase us out?' It did seem unfair, especially if I think that in the drawer of my bedside table in the best hotel in Lagos instead of the usual Bible I found an elegant pack of condoms in a box bearing the logo of the hotel, as if they were a bar of soap or a shower cap.

Another big worry for Nigerians was forged tickets. To avoid problems the organisers had decided to have the tickets printed in England. So far, so good. Except that the tickets for the inaugural match, Nigeria v Costa Rica, due to be played in Lagos, arrived in the Nigerian capital only the day before the game. So they went on sale on the Saturday morning, just hours before the game, which attracted almost 50,000 spectators. Impossibly long queues were controlled by mounted policemen armed with long whips. When we got to the Surulere, the stadium which takes its name from the neighbourhood in which it is situated, I saw at first hand what was happening to anyone trying to jump the queue: indiscriminate lashes straight out of Indiana Jones that struck virtually everybody, even people who were queuing in an orderly fashion. The crowd would sway, break up, then re-form, people cursing and swearing as they resumed the long wait for tickets. Corporal punishment and a threatening, exaggerated use of force are part of the picture in this part of the world.

Returning from the stadium to our hotel in Enugu, our minibus had its side door open. We were in no hurry but to get pedestrians out of the way as fast as possible, the bodyguard who was there to protect us (I am unsure from what as the atmosphere was totally laid-back) was hitting any poor soul within arm's reach on the back of the head with the butt of his pistol. I was travelling with a group of Portuguese journalists and we all told the bodyguard to leave the people alone, to stop it, but he went on and on. The victims themselves did not seem to mind, though – no one complained.

Things had gone well at the airport, but a nasty surprise was in store in the hotel. Not so much – or not only – on account of the prices, which in some cases had increased by 800 per cent, but because of a curious and potentially ruinous detail. In every hotel in Nigeria, you pay (or used to pay) in advance, not just the price of your room but at least 50 per cent extra, and on checkout you would be refunded the unused amount. Fair enough, just a pity that in those days you could only pay by credit card in a few places (though, since frauds major and minor were so common, sensible people always advised against it) and you could not pay in currency other than the local naira. The highest denomination was the 50 naira note, the equivalent of 50p. Imagine what it would mean to pay £250 in 50p pieces. You could change money at hotels or on the black market, in dodgy dives near the airport, and you went out with envelopes full of cash.

FIFA had concentrated all its efforts on Lagos, which had been converted temporarily into a spa for the elderly. The heat was unbearable but if you followed the hosts' guidelines you risked nothing, one reason being that they made you travel in cars marked VVIP. Very Very Important Persons. You cannot get much more important than that. Without our asking and without even telling us, the organisers had prepaid air tickets for Kaduna waiting for us. Single tickets, because they were not responsible for the return flight from a city out of their control.

In the other seven cities chosen to host the matches in the tournament, and thus to ensure money for different regions, anarchy reigned. Outside Lagos you did not run any great danger, but racketeering was rife: everybody wanted to exploit the Cup somehow and the poor FIFA delegates sent far away from the big city found themselves in situations that would have been hilarious if they had not risked nervous break-downs. Enugu is a small hill town with up and down streets, surrounded and lined with Caribbean-like tropical vegetation and a scourge of grass-hoppers that at dusk moved in *en masse*, forcing the referee to suspend temporarily the Mali v Portugal match. It was here that the Nigerian head official wanted journalists to pay admission to the ground. The FIFA delegate tried to make him see reason but he succeeded only to a point. It is true that journalists were eventually allowed in free but the head of the press office removed the two TV sets from the international press room. 'If they are watching the match live,' he explained, 'they don't need television.' The two sets ended up in his office, naturally enough.

In Kaduna, the former capital of the north of the country, a Muslim stronghold swept by the *harmattan*, a wind capable of blowing an artificial mist of prickly dust that stuck to your skin and got into your throat, exorbitant sums were extorted from the journalists in the press office. Forget about the free air tickets, just to receive a fax you had to pay the equivalent of nearly £3 a page. To send a fax, as in all other stadiums in Nigeria, you had to pay a three-minute minimum, about £10, even if you only wanted to send a page. After the first week, the head of FIFA in Kaduna managed to have the toll taken off incoming faxes but not to explain to the city's zealous pen-pushers how the internet worked. To connect to the web cost 50p a minute – half the amount we were asked for initially – because it was necessary to pay for the link from Nigeria to Europe or South America. Every effort to explain that the connection was local and not international, that you were linked with Kaduna not Buenos Aires, was in vain. Nothing doing. It was also complicated to use the telephones and there were no written instructions. You learned by experience and cash – the money spent to acquire the know-how – that once you had dialled a number, if and when you heard a friendly voice at the other end of the line, you then had to press a button. Otherwise the conversation was one-way: you could hear but you couldn't speak.

There were also comic sides to the affair. As soon as he arrived in Kaduna, the Ghana centre-forward Peter Ofori Quaye called his manager, Beppe Dossena, urgently. 'I can't go to the toilet,' he said. Worried about his player's health, Dossena went up to his room with him. In the toilet he found a 'window' of about a square metre with no glass, basically a square hole in the wall. Outside was a group of girls waiting faithfully and with a certain degree of wishful thinking for the player to perform his vital functions, hoping to see him naked. Argentina stayed in Lagos for two days in a hotel without electricity or water. After landing in the city, Kazakhstan missed their connection to Kaduna, where they were supposed to play their qualifying matches, and were stuck for two days without being able to train.

During the first match in the tournament in Ibadan with Blatter present in the stands, the lights suddenly went off. They came back on after 20 minutes but the next day five people were arrested. Poor souls: the local electricity board clerks had nothing to do with the mishap but somebody had to pay.

Nigeria represents everything bad about Africa: corruption, widespread poverty, vice, military dictatorship, violence. But it also possesses immense human, cultural and productive resources; great creativity, intelligence and talent. The same applies to its football. In general the Nigerians, together with their neighbours from Cameroon, are the best on the continent. The best in terms of skill and attitude, capable of travelling to the most far flung destinations and adapting without major problems. Just think of the tour organised by a representative side to England in the 1950s, when the Nigerians played barefoot in winter against opponents wearing normal boots. The Nigerians were protected then as now by a thick armour of versatility and matchless spirit.

It is just a pity they are incapable of organising a decent championship. To think that they qualified for the World Cup finals for the first time as recently as 1994, and that they have won the African Cup of Nations only twice (1980 and 1994), whereas Egypt and Ghana have won six and four times respectively. Their first victory in the African Champions Cup, for club sides, came in 2003. It is because the finest talents all leave (about a thousand Nigerian footballers play abroad at every level), because when they go home, call-ups for the national team are more an excuse to be with their friends than anything else and because internecine power struggles in the federation or among the players themselves for tribal, economic and religious motives have always caused terrible damage.

In Lagos there is a place that defines the reality of football in the country to perfection: raw and abundant talent, hopes, disappointments, frauds, dreams, few means but plenty of desire. Evans Square in the Oniyngbo neighbourhood is almost a round-the-clock gym. Obafemi Martins, to cite just one name, built his reputation there. So did his old mate Benjamin Onwuachi, less fortunate than him in Europe, who signed for Juventus but is now at SK Tirana in Albania. Here young football mercenaries come to offer their services to teams that are formed in the morning and break up in the evening, to play in tournaments and attempt to earn the odd naira from match bonuses and bets. A British director shot a film called *The Game of Life* here.

A soft-hard sandy field, crumbling two-metre-high beige brick walls on three sides, on which spectators huddle together, broken down goals, oven-like temperatures, a volatile climate, very brave referees and murderous tackling. Plus talent, exceptional talent. It's called *Jeunjeun*, pay-to-play football. Each single player tries to build a reputation but without tying himself permanently to a single team. He sells his skills to the highest bidder to take some cash home. Maximum 500 nairas (just over £3) a match, 10,000 (£60 or so) for the whole team, if the betting gets heavy. Not that these earnings are net: a percentage goes to an agent. For besides the players in Evans Square, there are also agents who 'sell' them and presidents who hire them. All the presidents have is the name of their team (Obafemi's was United Warriors) but they don't have a fixed side as the players are always on the market. The level of skill is very high, despite the somewhat wild atmosphere. Teams are picked on the spur of the moment, the playing surface is dreadful and tactics are conspicuous by their absence. It is here that African football gives its best.

9. A game for young men

At the stadium in Kaduna we start breathing again. The sun set an hour ago and, as if by magic, the *harmattan* has dropped. The stadium is half-deserted as Argentina and Kazakhstan prepare to meet in the second match in Group B of the Under-20 World Cup in Nigeria. The South Americans are champions of their own continent and two years earlier they won the Under-20 World Cup in Malaysia. Not that people in Kaduna care. Cambiasso? Milito? Rivarola? Galletti? Names that mean little to Nigerians, while the Kazakh names mean nothing at all. The match drags on and the Argentina captain Cambiasso scores the only goal. The highlight of the game comes halfway through the second half. From the central grandstand, where a hundred or so Nigerians are sitting, a spontaneous chant rises up: 'Argentina overage, Argentina overage' – a masterpiece of tongue-in-cheek irony. The chant goes on for a while, as the Nigerians enjoy the chance to call the South Americans cheats, to return criticisms about the alleged ages of African players and the passport fixing that goes on in world youth competitions. The Argentines pay no attention and the Kazakhs couldn't give a damn, but the episode in itself is a symbol. At least for me.

In all likelihood, the Argentines aren't 'overage' at all. But the fact that the Nigerians rib them so mercilessly, thereby making public a subject previously considered taboo in Africa, is, to say the least, curious and highly indicative of the boundless cheek of Nigerians.

At this point, it is worth taking a short step backwards. In 1981 I was 14 and an enthusiastic Internazionale fan. I was particularly struck by a passport scandal in which my team was involved. To do well in a prestigious international Under-16 tournament, Inter decided to field Massimo Pellegrini, a youngster considered a likely star of the future, under the name of a team-mate, Massimo Ottolenghi. Pellegrini was overage for the competition but Ottolenghi was eligible. Inter did what we used to do with suspended players in the minor leagues in Rome – we came up with another player's documents. When the referee came to check your identity, if you were self-confident enough, all you had to do was to give a false surname then turn round quick enough to hide your face and let him check your number and studs. I had seen this happen many a time on pitches in the northern suburbs of Rome. Yet the Inter affair remained imprinted in my memory. Partly because I still had not started to play but, above all, because I could not understand why they did such a thing. Cheating to win an Under-16 tournament? Poor Inter.

Years later, when I was compiling my African annuals, I had to address the problem of dodgy passports. It took some investigating to get to the bottom of things. That African national teams alter the passports of their players in youth competitions is an established fact. It is rare for anyone to be caught, though. What connects the story of Massimo Pellegrini to that of many African youngsters is the significance that a 'rejuvenated' passport can have. Pellegrini was seen as being so good that Inter reckoned it was worth risking making fools of themselves internationally. But he subsequently played only one match in Serie A. Maybe he wasn't so great after all. Or maybe he just lost his way. Many African kids come to Europe with passports that seem advantageous for their careers but on many occasions those documents turn into burdens.

Coming to Europe at 15, 16, 17 years of age, they normally end up playing with other kids – with the youth team if they are lucky, the schoolboys if they are not. In Europe the idea is deep-rooted that the African footballer is tactically naive, that he needs to mature. The prejudice is even stronger when applied to youngsters of 16. And so their apprenticeship begins. A young man of 20 to 22 finds himself living and playing with boys. In Africa he may already have a wife and kids, but in Europe he has to play the role of the adolescent. As if it was not hard enough for him to change city, country, continent, eating and social habits, language, friends, affections. Many don't make it.

Psychologically and technically, it is easy to stand out playing against people who are five or six years younger than you. But at the same time you do not improve your game. You may be at the peak of your career but your employers, the people with your future in their hands, think you are a kid and you end up stagnating. So you fail to exploit the main opportunities when you are called up to the first team. You get depressed and go backwards, on loan to smaller and smaller clubs. There are many such sad stories, some of them with very unhappy endings.

Of course, if you are really good you make headway. Sometimes you can negotiate fabulous contracts with the help of a generous passport. But at the end of their careers, when they are on the wane, some African players go out like matches, all of a sudden. I am thinking of certain Nigerians in particular, though I know nothing about their passports. Finidi George, for example, a European champion with Ajax who ended up at Ipswich Town in the English second level at 30 and finished his career at 31. Or Taribo West, whose last full championship was the one he lost with Inter against Juventus in Turin in 1998, when he was only 24. He has since only made sporadic appearances here and there round the world, in England, Germany, Serbia, Qatar and England again. At 31 he was sold by Plymouth Argyle in the English second tier and in August 2007 he signed a one-year contract with Iranian club Paykan FC. Or Victor Ikpeba, three great seasons with Monaco between 1996, when he was 26, and 1999; hardly anything since. Or Daniel Amokachi, whose career ended at the age of 27. Or Tijani Babangida, who played his last decent season for Ajax in 1999, when he was 25. There are many other such examples in many other countries.

In Cameroon two cases come to mind, those of Salomon Olembé and Tobie Mimboe Bayard, the latter a man who never has a birthday. Olembé, still a member of the national team, has a passport that was issued in 1980, but he played for many years in France, England and Saudi Arabia. After a couple of years with Olympique de Marseille, he signed for Wigan Athletic in 2007. In the 1998 African Cup of Nations in Burkina Faso, Olembé, a left-back, was officially 17. He played well and with Italy due to play Cameroon in the World Cup a few months later, he attracted the attention of the Italian press. After one match we stopped him and asked him to tell us his story. I was the interpreter. After two or three minutes hearing him run off his CV – 'I played here, I played there' – I interrupted him and suggested that he'd had quite a career for a 17-year-old. He smiled and said nothing about the most recent years in a prodigious career that had only just begun. Olembé had arrived in France, at Nantes, in 1990. At that stage he was technically ten years old. There's a rumour that he was actually born in December 1973. That sounds much more realistic. Salomon would now appear to be 27 and to have 11 seasons in Europe under his belt (plus, presumably, a couple in Africa). The last season in which he was picked as a first team starter in more than 20 matches was 2000-01.

Mimboe Bayard belongs to the creative school, one of those who change their passports according to season and opportunity. At the 1996 African Cup of Nations, he turned up with a document which, under Date of Birth, read June 30, 1964. After the disappointing performance of the Indomitable Lions and consequent difficulties in finding a contract abroad, he decided to tweak his passport – Date of Birth June 30, 1970. The new document yielded the result he was hoping for and Mimboe left for Argentina. Then he moved to Paraguay, where he signed for Cerro Porteño. But Europe is Europe and the gritty midfielder did some more trimming. The result of the handiwork was that his birthday was still June 30, but his date of birth had shifted to 1974. Ten years younger in two trims. Thanks to this phenomenal document, Tobie won over the directors of Genclerbirligi, in Turkey. Now that he had a new contract, maybe out of a sense of common decency, for the African Cup of Nations in 1998 Mimboe decided to produce the intermediate passport (the 1970 one) out of his drawer.

It would be wrong to overlook African manners, modes and mores. Claude Le Roy, the French manager with much experience in Africa, once told me that, many years ago at Douala airport, he had bumped into Thomas Nkono, the Cameroon national team goalkeeper. He was with a bright little kid of two or three. 'I'm off to the registry office,' Nkono told Le Roy, 'to register my son.'

Nii Odartey Lamptey, one of the many 'new Pelés' who have appeared in the recent past, deserves a special mention. Some Roma fans may remember him running rings round their defenders for Anderlecht in a UEFA Cup match in 1990-91. He was 16 at the time. Lamptey won the Under-17 World Cup in Montecatini, Italy, with Ghana in 1991. He played phenomenally. He was a phenomenon. Before Montecatini, he had played one full season with Anderlecht, scoring seven goals in 14 matches. After Montecatini, a void. Then came a fleeting reappearance with PSV Eindhoven two years later, when he was 19 or 20, then oblivion again. But it was a colourful oblivion, one that could fill a guidebook for three continents outside Africa, featuring spells in England (Aston Villa, Coventry City), Italy, Turkey, Argentina, Portugal, Germany and China.

His fame as the 'new Pelé' had faded, but not enough to prevent 'young' Lamptey from signing contracts all around the world. In 2000 in Accra I got a ride from a young taxi driver. He must have been 20, 25 at the most. He saw I had an African Cup of Nations accreditation pass round my neck, and we got to talking about football. He was well informed. Our long chat culminated with a *coup de théâtre*. 'I'm Lamptey's son,' he said. I burst out laughing, but he insisted. I will never know the truth but the taxi driver was adamant and my unwillingness to believe his confession obviously hurt him.

I repeat, I have nothing to reveal about the passports of the players I have mentioned. But their rapid decline is, to say the least, sensational. When I began to collect data for my first annual, I found three cases of Nigerian internationals who had played in two different FIFA competitions with passports bearing different dates of birth. When Augustine Eguavoen, a former manager of Nigeria, went to the Seoul Olympics his date of birth was in 1961, but when he went to the World Cup in 1994 it had shifted to 1965. Samson Siasia, now coach of Nigeria's Under-20s, went from 1964 to 1967 at the same two competitions. And Rashidi Yekini, the 'bull of Kaduna', who became famous for praying in the goal after scoring against Bulgaria at the 1994 World Cup, went from 1962 to 1964. All this information is documented in the technical reports published by FIFA.

It was no coincidence that the Seoul Olympics should cost Nigeria dearly. The secretary in charge of footballers' passports, a very delicate role in African federations, was obviously no magician. Or maybe by dint of changing, adjusting, retouching and filing documents, he'd got mixed up. Whatever the case, three players – Dahiru Sadi, Samson Siasia (him again) and Andrew Uwe – turned up in South Korea with dates of birth that were different from the ones they had used in previous FIFA competitions. The Nigerian federation had decided to surprise everyone but its clever move turned into an own goal. The three players in the Seoul squad had got older, not younger. Dahiru, born in 1965 for the Under-20 World Cup in Mexico 1983, had now been born in 1963. It was like the story of the film *Cocoon* told in reverse. Uwe aged as much as four years, moving from 1967 (in the passport used in Russia in 1985 for another Under-20 World Cup) to 1963. Siasia went back from 1967 to 1964. Then, as we have seen, he resorted to 1967 for the USA 94, when a couple of good performances might have ensured him a new contract in Europe. FIFA were annoyed and banned Nigeria from all youth competitions for two years.

In November 2006, Carlos Alberto of Figueirense in Brazil, a member of the Brazil team that beat Spain in the final of the 2003 Under-20 World Cup in the United Arab Emirates, confessed he had lowered his age by five years (changing his year of birth from 1978 to 1983) to be able to take part. He said he did it 'out of hunger' and assumed all responsibility for his actions, thus freeing his club and the Brazilian federation from blame. He was suspended for one year but, despite protests from Spain, no action was taken against Brazil. It was a case of double standards compared with Africa, but also with Mexico, expelled from the Seoul Olympics and the 1990 World Cup finals for falsifying their players' passports.

All these numbers, examples and errors are just the start of it. In the meantime, the game in Africa has been positively influenced not so much by the FIFA ban (which, apart from making federations more careful in their document fiddling, achieved no result whatsoever) as by the outcries of two politicians: the Nigerian Minister of Sport and Social Development, Steven Ibn Akiga, and the Ghanaian Deputy Minister of Sport and Youth, Joe Aggrey. At the start of 2003, just days apart, Akiga and Aggrey stated publicly that everyone in Nigeria and Ghana knew what was going on, though they claimed not to, and that the successes of their nations' youth teams had been made possible by the scientific falsification of passports.

Before joining the government, Aggrey had been a highly respected journalist. After graduating, he had travelled abroad with his country's various youth teams. 'Ghana have cheated in the past, and are now bearing the fruits of seeds sown some years ago,' he said. 'In the past, we were cheating and winning, but the right thing must be done now. The plans of the government to develop a new youth policy is welcome. Years of lopsided policies, which put a premium on juvenile football, have adversely affected the standards of the senior national team, the Black Stars.' It's true – Ghana, winners of the Under-17 World Cup in 1991, of the first African medal in Olympic football with a bronze in Barcelona in 1992, a competition then reserved for Under-23 teams, second at the Under-20 World Cup in 1993, first, second and third at the Under-17

World Cups in 1995, 1997 and 1999 respectively, had never qualified for the real World Cup, the one for 'grown-ups'.

Why had the vast majority of those kids never made it to the top? Why had all those boy geniuses disappeared? The problem was that those players had reached their peak when, according to their passports, they were still wet behind the ears. Talent seemed to wane with the passage from puberty (or at least the puberty certified in their documents) to adulthood, but maybe things are changing now. At the Under-17 World Cups in 2003 and 2005, the six African sides that competed were all eliminated in the first round. In 2007, however, Nigeria won the tournament and Ghana came fourth after losing the semi-final after extra time. Today Ghana even qualify for the real World Cup. Maybe the policy launched by Aggrey is bearing fruit.

'We have for a while now been fielding players far above the ages agreed for some international age group competitions,' declared Akiga, a former footballer and hockey player. 'This has not helped our football and we must now fight against these age cheats.' A Nigerian minister had never spoken so openly about the problem because governments had always tacitly approved a 'victory at all costs' policy. Because, in Africa as elsewhere, football is a panacea. When Ghana won the Under-17 World Cup in Montecatini, President Jerry Rawlings was hosting a gathering of 84 ministers from as many non-aligned countries. All the meetings scheduled were cancelled and two days of national celebrations were declared. A million Ghanaians went to Accra airport to welcome home their heroes, led by Lamptey, named the best player in the competition. Everyone knew the tournament had been won with the help of the odd altered passport but had decided to forget about it in the name of national unity and glory.

'In a country of over 250 ethnic groups bound together only when any of the national teams are playing, it is hard to countenance losing grip of an event that was so much under the belt, or talk of a programme that would discountenance 'winning-at-all-cost,' wrote one journalist in the Nigerian national daily *Vanguard*. Nigeria won the first Under-16 World Cup in China in 1985, losing the next one in Canada on penalties. 'The question to ask is: where are all those good, great players?' said *Vanguard*. 'Most of them have burnt out, ambushed by age at a time they were expected to be reaching their peak! In 1983, just as the Under-20 team was about to leave for Mexico for the FIFA world youth championship, a scandal broke over the fact that some players were above the age limit. Consequently the team captain, Charity Ikhidero, among others, was dropped. Amazingly, the same Charity Ikhidero (may his soul rest in peace) was repackaged as Tunde Charity in 1989 for the same age-grade competition. That was six years after he was discovered to be too old for the same level!'

Vanguard's exposé was precise and circumspect. But also sensational. The player also turned out in the no-age-limit five-a-side World Cup in Hong Kong in 1992, on that occasion with the double surname of Ikhidero-Charity. He died in September 1997, following a clash of heads in a first division match between Insurance of Benin City, his team, and Nigerdock of Lagos. Judging by the passport he used in Saudi Arabia he was 26. Realistically, he was probably ten years or so older.

In the summer of 2005, I unwittingly caused a scandal to explode in Nigerian football. I was looking for information on the Nigerian federation website when I noted that the then Inter player Obafemi Martins (now with Newcastle) had suddenly aged six years.

> Speaking about strikers, a correction is due from the Nigerian federation: on its official site, accessible by a direct link from the FIFA federations page, the NFA gives Obafemi Martins' date of birth as May 1, 1978. In the *Panini Almanack*, however, the striker is six years younger, allegedly born on October 28, 1984. It is probably an error but confusion reigns.

It only took these few lines in the *Corriere della Sera* for all hell to break loose. The news was picked up by other papers and it reached Nigeria when I, the perpetrator of the scoop, was interviewed by the BBC. Obafemi was annoyed and demanded explanations. The NFA president Ibrahim Galadima proceeded to do just that, salvaging relations with his best player by blaming the site webmaster.

The poor guy was traced and arrested at dawn. He was then thrown into a cell and left there until he revealed the password to access the NFA site. He was the only person who knew it. It was a precious secret, at least for him. Though he was not exactly a paragon of professionalism (many other players had given wrong dates of birth and examples of 'cutting and pasting' repeated themselves all over the site) the webmaster was owed a considerable sum by the NFA. After asking for the money for months, in March he lost patience. Out of principle, he refused to reveal the site's password. Nobody noticed the error. When, thanks to *Corriere della Sera*, the scandal broke, the disgrace became world news and the webmaster became public enemy number one. And because football is such a serious business, he had to pay the price. Minister Akiga's accusations about tampering with passports were one thing, but you do not joke with the age of national team players. For a while, the site was not updated but then the international squad list disappeared, along with the double age of Obafemi Martins. The search is now on for a new webmaster.

10. At the roots of tourism

The lift in the Novotel in Accra is packed. The occupants are black or of mixed race, but they are not Ghanaian. They have strong American accents. They are all discreetly elegant in expensive casual and formal wear. It turns out that they are Americans and they are in Ghana on 'roots' tourism, in search of their origins. They do tours of forts, prisons and harbours, the places where their ancestors used to be locked up before being shipped off in chains to America. In Accra alone there are three forts, one each built by the British, Dutch and Danish. In the 18th century, there were as many as 38 in the country. Today some have been cleaned up and converted into hotels.

It sounds like a rather macabre, morbid sort of tourism to me. One reason for this is that some of the tourists do not seem entirely at peace with the colour of their skin and their desire to stand out from the locals is tangible. It is a sensation as precise and strong as their American accents. They seem to be asking their African brothers for respect – and distance. When I went to Cape Coast, a small town on the ocean, northeast of Accra, to take a look at a pitch where a local tournament was to be played, I found the same Americans in the fort that was the main muster point for slaves on the way out of the Gold Coast, as the country was known until 1957. They didn't seem to like being there. Theirs was not a journey of social protest, of anger and memory – they seemed confused and unconvinced.

I have been to Ghana several times. For the Under-20 Cup of Nations and for the real Cup of Nations, to report on the progress of the former Torino and Sampdoria player Beppe Dossena as coach of various national teams, then I watched the Germany 2006 second-round game between Ghana and Brazil in Accra. It is a welcoming country, in no way dangerous; enjoyable, quiet, organised, open to tourists. What the country lacks is a touch of personality. As do its footballers. They do not possess the determination of players from Cameroon, Nigeria and Ivory Coast or the creativity of those from Burkina Faso and Senegal. Ghana is probably the most European of the African countries I have visited. In 2006 the national team, the Black Stars, reached the World Cup finals for the first time. Theirs had previously been a success story, but only in Africa – something had always been missing, preventing them from shining on the broader stage. The same applied to the footballers themselves: Abedi Pelé, a European champion with Marseille against AC Milan, Tony Yeboah, Samuel Kuffour, another European champion with Bayern Munich, but no one else. They had always shown lots of promise but always seemed to fall inches from the finishing post.

The country conveys the same sensation. Lots of potential, fewer glaring contrasts than in other African countries and an overall peacefulness that makes any stay in a place that gave the world a secretary of the United Nations very agreeable. The rise and election of Kofi Annan were a bolt from the blue. That and the difficulties created for Annan by his son in the Oil for Food scandal – in which various people and organisations profited from the illicit sale of Iraqi oil – capture the essence of Ghana, in 1957 the first African country to gain independence, thanks to the political genius of Kwame Nkrumah, another great leader whose example has been followed by very few.

In Ghana they don't know how to say No. It is a characteristic shared by many other African nations but here it is more marked. They never want to disappoint or appear impolite. Since the country functions relatively smoothly, they reckon they can cope. Sometimes they perform miracles, other times they create problems out of nothing. Taxi drivers are not out to make money at all costs. They are honest and if they strike an agreement, they keep their word. They turn on the meter when you sit down in the taxi and, in the majority of cases, it does not spin round like a 78rpm record, a common vice in north Africa. Sometimes, alas, their knowledge of the city is limited, normally because they already do other jobs and their mate has lent them the taxi for the weekend to supplement their income. So as not to appear unprofessional, the driver always tells you that he knows where he is going. He thinks it is unseemly to ask for information. Unless, that is, he bumps into a mate at a traffic light, in which case he can speak in his own language (if he were to speak in English I would understand he has no idea where we are going). Getting to the Nigerian embassy in Accra for a visa was always a long, drawn-out operation. Aside from the difficulties involved in contacting the visa office and coping with the Nigerian staff, arriving in Tito Avenue (international statesmen, from Nehru to Nasser, are popular in Accra street names) was a major feat. You always got lost. 'Do you know where the embassy is?' I used to ask. 'Yes, sir,' they always answered. It was untrue and we would embark on an epic voyage round the quiet green residential neighbourhood that hosted this outpost of Nigeria.

On a couple of occasions I had to go to see matches in Kumasi, the second city. It is 250 kilometres from Accra and it takes four to five hours by road, depending on the driver and the car. The journey is unadvisable by night: there is not a single street lamp along the way and there is a high chance of running over men or animals or into objects that have fallen off the back of lorries. The first time I went to Kumasi, I took the plane, having been offered a ticket at a bargain price. When I asked for information about domestic flight operators at the hotel (Ghana Airways, the national airline, only operates internationally) a keen Novotel clerk told me to rely on him. I decided to behave like a Ghanaian and did not say no. I paid half the fee at once and waited for further instructions. The day before my departure I still had no ticket. The clerk was called Kodjo, quite a common name, because he had been born on a Monday. According to Ewe tradition, every day of the week corresponds to a name for boys and a name for girls. If you are born on Saturday, you are called Kwame, on Thursday Yaw, on Friday Kofi, and so on. Kodjo wanted the balance for the ticket but since mine was a day return, and I had nothing to go on but his word, I told him I would pay when I got back to Accra. A long, friendly negotiation ensued and it ended with a victory for the away team. For me, that is.

On the morning of the journey, I had a taxi booked for 6am because I had to be at the airport half an hour later. This time Kodjo had organised and lectured the driver. He would take me to the right place. The sky was blue and the streets were deserted. Before arriving at the airport, my man turned right, then left towards the military airport. I asked for an explanation and he told me to trust him. Regular as clockwork, a guard stopped us. There were hardly any cars in the area so our arrival required some form of justification. The driver explained and the guard was satisfied. It was a placid conversation: in Cameroon or Nigeria I would never have got past without handing over some cash. Near a large hangar we turned left. We drove the length of the hangar and then stopped. End of the run. I got out and walked round the corner, where I saw a small solid private plane on the runway. I also saw a cluster of 20 or so people: the Minister of Sport, the president of the football federation, a couple of senior military dignitaries and a few other famous faces from the Ghanaian football-political establishment.

My driver approached one of the military men, spoke to him and pointed at me. The man nodded. My driver then came back to me, bade me farewell and promised to come to pick me up that evening. I was dressed in a black Jamaica T-shirt with a number seven on the back and a pair of dark red Bermuda shorts. I would have been the coolest in the group if it had been a skateboarding session but my look was decidedly weird for the presidential aeroplane. I was second on board and I made myself comfortable in the biggest seat, actually more like a settee than a seat. When the minister arrived, I realised that I was sitting in his place. I moved – to another excellent seat, let it be said. Sixteen of the 30 or so seats on the plane were arranged in the classic manner in four rows at the back, the others were scattered round the 'lounge'. There was a space in the middle with a stylish mahogany bar on one side and a huge television set into the wood panelling on the other.

It was the personal plane of President Jerry Rawlings, the army colonel who had risen to power after a coup in the late 1970s. The plane had a Seventies feel to it, like something out of a James Bond film. There was upholstery and wood in varying shades of brown, true vintage elegance. Unfortunately, though they tolerated my presence, I was told that photographs were forbidden. It was the same at the airport, the customs office and the army barracks. The plane was protected by official secrecy. No problem. I thought about ordering martini as James Bond would have done, looked at my watch and opted for a Coca-Cola, which was served by a very smart waiter. It was a journey for gentlemen.

My second trip to Kumasi, a year later, was inevitably less exclusive than the first. There was no plane and Kodjo was nowhere to be found (maybe they sacked him for getting me onto the presidential plane) so I decided to go by car with a Roman photographer and his girlfriend. We went down to the Neoplan station, near the roundabout named after Nkrumah, and as soon as we entered the car park we were surrounded by a cluster of people – 'ticket clerks' and their agents. In the dusty clearing everything seemed uniformly ochre yellow, from the ground to the cars to the clothes. The place was packed with people waiting to set off. The 'fast cars' for Kumasi – broken down Peugeots that still manage to go faster than the minibuses, many of which are still made of wood – are known as *tro-tros* and leave only when they are full, seven passengers each. Some of the vehicles have smashed windscreens, others transport men and goats, others still are apparently packed to capacity but still wait for one last passenger to meet the agreed price. Everyone has a newer car to offer, or a faster, more experienced driver, or less damaged seats or an earlier departure time. In this bedlam of shouting and shrieking and offers you can't refuse and outstretched hands, a relatively distinguished young man steps forward and repeats three words – 'Good German car' – over and over again.

Only a few minutes have passed but I am already exhausted. I decide to trust him. His competitors realise good business – three Europeans – is slipping away from them and they double their efforts. We refuse to give in to them and follow the man of the three words. We walk past many battered Peugeots and suddenly there in front of us is an almost new silver BMW M3. It really is a 'good German car'. The price, very low to start with, is risible for a car like this. We sit down in the leather seats, the air-conditioning goes on and we hear the explanation. Kwabena works as a driver for a German businessman who lives in Kumasi. That morning he had taken his boss to Accra airport and now he was going home. Finding himself in town, he had decided to earn a bit of extra cash by picking up some passengers.

I have had the pleasure of training with the Ghana Under-20 team many times. When they did sprints at 60 per cent of their full capacity, I would lose three or four metres in every ten to them. We would train at 8am before it got too hot at the stadium in Accra or on the bald pitch in Kaduna, in Nigeria. I also attended many tactical and skill-training sessions as a spectator. Many of the players were already in Europe, others were still playing at home, waiting to make the big move. They were mild-mannered, modest, kind young men. The reserve goalkeeper was the prayer leader and was known as 'pastor'. He never took the field but everyone went to him and entrusted themselves to him for pre-match prayers. There were players who were phenomenal in training but stayed on the bench and suffered because of this. Then there was the joker and the respected captain to whom everybody listened, the hard worker who helped create group spirit and the shy striker who kept himself to himself. The difference between them, skill apart, was in their desire to reach the top, to change their lives. When the coach Dossena spoke, the brightest among them would listen, attentive and engrossed, aware of the fact that every word, every tip, every lesson could help them make the leap.

Mohammed Gargo was one of the three Ghanaians (the others were Samuel Kuffour and Emmanuel Duah) who joined Torino after Ghana won the Under-17 World Cup in Italy in 1991. They could not be signed officially because they were not European Union citizens but the Torino chairman Gianmauro Borsano hired them as messenger boys for his company, GIMA. The news got out and turned into an international scandal. The president of the Italian football association, Antonio Matarrese, spoke of a new slave trade. The three youngsters were sad, not because they felt like slaves but rather because they simply wanted to play football. They wanted to come to Italy at all costs and the move to Turin had brought their families a lot of money – huge sums by Ghanaian standards. After their sensational but controversial arrival in Europe, the three travelled around and ended up settling down: Gargo in Italy, Kuffour in Germany (then in Italy), Duah in Portugal.

In 1998 Gargo ruptured his knee ligaments playing for Ghana in the African Cup of Nations. He did not even notice at the time, staying on the field until the end of the game and walking round the next day without crutches. He was operated on in Rome at Villa Stuart, the clinic in the Balduina neighbourhood whose gardens bordered on my old primary school. I often visited him – in Rome he knew no one – and he used to tell me about himself. He sometimes got emotional. The posh clinic on the north side of Rome where he was being treated was a long way from his home town of Tamale.

When Gargo realised he could earn money through football, he had pushed himself to the limit. His family was very poor and very large. The first prize he won was a pair of football boots. He went home very happy and left them on the table. He knew he would never see them again, that they would get sold to supplement the family income. Gargo's father asked for nothing; it was a question of respect. His son said nothing, again out of respect. The same was true of cash prizes, which are regularly awarded on suburban pitches in Ghana and Nigeria. When Gargo told these stories, with his leg in traction and his gaze lost through the window, his eyes would fill with tears. Which is why the $80,000 Torino paid the Gargo family was a godsend. In Tamale, that sort of sum could set up entire generations.

When I returned to Accra in 2006 I found that it had grown out of all proportion, as if it had undergone unchecked hormone treatment. Some of the new buildings were made of cement but most were shacks and huts. The traffic was hell but the city was still placid, tranquil, reassuring. On Thursday June 22, 2006, the Ghana v USA and Brazil v Japan World Cup matches in Germany produced the results that everyone had been hoping for and Ghana would play Brazil in the last 16. I sent an email to the editor of the *Gazzetta dello Sport* suggesting a hare-brained journey. I wanted to go Accra to see this historic encounter at the home of one of the stars of Ghana's first World Cup team. The editor agreed immediately but then the problems started. I had moved to Madrid a month and a half earlier. The match was scheduled for the following Tuesday, so there was only one working day (Friday) to get a visa from an embassy that normally takes a fortnight or so to issue them.

Thanks to the intervention of a friend at the Italian embassy, the very kind Ghanaian attaché worked a miracle and on Sunday I was on the plane: Madrid-Milan-Lagos-Accra. The first obstacle came at Malpensa as an accident with a catering trolley had put the whole plane out of action. A new plane was needed and had to come from Rome. So a plane was coming from the south to the north to take us from the north to the south while we sat and waited, for five hours. I eventually landed in Accra on the Monday, at dawn. There was humidity, greyness and warm, damp air. The dry heat of Madrid was a pleasant memory.

Before leaving I had been in touch with Stephen Appiah, nicknamed 'Tornado'. The Ghana captain promised to arrange for me to watch the match with his mother and cousins. I had slept for only a few hours but I had to spend the whole of the Monday organising the day to come. Kwabena Ofori, the photographer who was supposed to be my guardian, was in Germany following the Black Stars but he left me in the care of his assistant, the Cameroonian Pierre Toto, whom I had already met during my travels in Africa. Pierre caught up with me at the offices of the most important daily in Accra, the *Daily Graphic*. After giving a couple of interviews and being photographed (a European journalist arriving in town to follow the game was a big event) we hop into a car with Sam Akenteng, a veteran sports reporter, and set off seawards. They tell me they will try to contact Appiah's mother but in the meantime we go looking for his cousin Francis, who still lives in the ocean-side slum of Chorkor.

It was with the arrival of fishermen here that the expansion of Accra into the giant it is today began. For locals, this is the true centre of town and it is here that the captain was born. 'He's a true Brazilian,' say Appiah's cousins, 'because in Chorkor the kids play soccer on the beach all day, just like they do on the other side of the ocean.' Appiah's father does not live in Accra and his mother has moved into the big house Stephen bought in one of the city's residential neighbourhoods. His cousins have stayed on here, though, in the 'Appiah family house', as the locals proudly call it. Our first stop is at a 'bathing establishment': a few ramshackle deckchairs, a nice terrace for dancing, wood tables ruined by the salt air and the wind, a sleepy bar and only a handful of punters on account of the unfavourable climate and the still less favourable hour.

We wait for the 'connection' who is supposed to take us to Francis. After an hour or so, two youngsters turn up. The five of us squeeze into Sam's sports car and set off along the seafront. I am confident. There has been no word about Mrs Appiah but the cousin could be just round the corner. Three or four kilometres with the sea on our left and shacks to our right, then a right turn, then a left turn and we arrive. Our destination is a plain cement house: a big cube with a sunblind and a small yard to the left. I meet to the cousin and we make arrangements for the next day. They are kind here but also sceptical: no one thinks that I am really going to come back and watch the match with them.

'*Obiaaa nye obiaaa*' (We're not frightened of anybody) is the most popular chant in Ghana. 'We're going to win because the Brazilians come from Africa and we know them well.' The World Cup has reawakened a dormant patriotism. 'Proud to be Ghanaian' stickers are everywhere, tricolours are draped on all the cars and flutter in a thousand shapes and sizes at traffic lights. Flags, whistles, hats, T-shirts, dresses, mobile phone holders all display the same word *Yetoaso* – 'Come On' in Twi, one of the local languages. At a crossroads in the Osu quarter, an area of busy restaurants and bars with giant screens, there is a 'human statue'.

He stands still for minutes on end, his body painted with yellow, green and red vertical stripes, then a black star, and further up the result: '2' below the word 'Ghana' on his left shoulder blade, with '0' under the word 'Brazil' on his right shoulder blade.

Tomorrow the big meeting point is in Independence Square, a huge unsurfaced esplanade with stands on all sides, where Bill Clinton drew 500,000 people in 1998. Here the whole of Accra is going to see the game on a giant screen set up in front of the ocean. At 3pm local time, when the match is due to kick off, there will be a tacit 'early closing' for civil servants, who usually stay in their offices until five. Behind the fans, a huge black star has been stuck on the monument that celebrates Ghana's independence in 1957.

Sam's wife had a shop, a little DVD rental place. The goods are all Nollywood, the African Bollywood. It is a genre in which every film has a sequel but never a third instalment. A few titles: *Blood Sister, Unknown Angel, Heaven Must Shake, Oh! Mother, Because of Love*. Sam, Pierre and I sit down to watch Italy v Australia, eating peanuts and drinking local beer. In Accra, the penalty which generously allows Italy to go through to the quarter-finals is judged to be daylight robbery. The comments are the same as in all the rest of the world: Italy are cynical, defensive and lucky. Mrs Akenteng calls us for dinner: hot spicy stew and white rice, which we eat with our hands. Goodbye till tomorrow.

The match is at 3pm but I tell them to come to collect me at 11am. We have to cross the city and the city is hit by uncontainable World Cup fever. Nobody comes. Sam has family problems, Pierre has vanished. I wait. At one o'clock, Sam turns up. An hour later we have driven no more than two kilometres and there are still at least another ten to go. Accra is one long queue. It is unlikely that all these people are going to get where they want to be in time for kick-off. But I am worried about the article I have to write. Having flown from Madrid to Accra, I do not want to hear the match on the car radio. Then I have a brainwave. I ask Sam to stop the first motorcyclist who comes by. I get lucky. The first is Kofi, on a grey 1960s Triumph. The bike is elegant in an old-fashioned way, with a Ghana flag over the front headlamp ('It's broken anyway!'). I tell Sam to start the bargaining. Kofi accepts the offer and I get out of the car and jump onto his motorbike. Sam and his wife look very worried. I have no helmet. I lean forward in aerodynamic mode, put my hands on my knees and tell my new friend not to worry. More than 30 years on a scooter in the Roman traffic have prepared me for almost anything. I squeeze my knees tight and we start to slip and slide through the standing cars. Kofi sees that I am comfortable and starts being more daring. Time passes and the traffic does not move.

Then there's the first problem: 'Do you know where we have to go?' Kofi asks. 'More or less,' I reply. 'Take me to the seafront and we'll work it out from there.' The ocean appears in front of us, the traffic thins out and Kofi gives his Triumph full throttle. My hair flies back in the wind, the speed brings tears to my eyes – it is like a commercial for a 1970s racing bike.

So I am in Chorkor, on the promenade, but I have to find the Appiah family house where was yesterday for the first and only time in my life. The houses are all the same, like the streets. I tell Kofi to go on. Then I remember the police barracks – tin roof, blue sign – and it all comes back to me when I spot a huge manhole cover sticking up at least 30 centimetres above the level of the road. I had seen it yesterday too. 'Next on the right.' Kofi trusts me, mainly because he hasn't much option. There are 15 minutes to kick-off. 'Second on the left.' We are there. When we appear, the street comes to life. The white man is going to support Ghana with all the rest of us. Francis approaches and introduces me to Salomon, another cousin. Salomon is wearing a white skullcap with yellow, red and green hoops, a yellow, green and black string vest and earrings, three tricolour balls per ear. He also has a big Ghana flag over his shoulders. The TV is a 20-inch Universum, set up on a table outside the house. A chair appears and I am asked to sit down. Next appears a red-and-blue umbrella, held by a young man: the rules of hospitality require that I sit with my head protected from the sun. I ask Kofi to stay and introduce him to the Black Stars captain's cousins. At this point I could ask him to take me to Madrid on his Triumph and he would willingly oblige. It is his lucky day. Who knows, maybe the Black Stars really will pull off a miracle?

At kick-off we are all crowded round the angular Universum – 20 or so children and as many adults. Old women with flags round their heads instead of scarves sit on a side bench. I'm in the VIP stand, with my chair in the most central position, just a couple of metres from the screen. The match starts and Ronaldo scores. Offside maybe? A lady comes all the way down the road with a huge tub on her head, splashing water everywhere as if to wash away the referee's sins. 'Thieves!' she says amid general laughter. Ghana then start to get into the game and hopes grow in the Appiah household. 'He's the real Brazilian,' shouts one of them when the captain touches the ball. A Ghanaian player attempts an overhead kick. He mistimes it, but here in Chorkor there is total admiration for his attempt. The continuous bickering gets more and more tense. The defence is wobbly and the panic increases. Every now and again a bare-chested man comes out of the house opposite and argues about fine points with anybody who can be bothered to answer him before going back in again. Somewhat optimistically, they shout for a goal when Dida miraculously saves John Mensah's header on the line but four minutes later Brazil's second goal comes as a body blow. Despondency all round. Confidence evaporates with the heat and mingles with the humidity. Cousin Salomon can't stand any more and leaves.

At half time it is the women who try to psyche up the rest as the men have already given up. From further down the road comes a group of women and girls singing and dancing. The rowdiest has a T-shirt with a large photo of Appiah and the slogan 'No Tornado, No Party'. Then three boys, their faces painted black, appear and improvise a march. It is time for me to pay back the generous hospitality. With the equivalent of €3 the messenger Francis sends to the bar comes back with 16 bottles of Coca-Cola. I think I should double the order.

The second half kicks off. A voice says 'Stephen plays better with Essien' (Michael is out suspended). They cheer Mensah ('immense'), they jeer Asamoah Gyan: 'You can't go to the World Cup with a striker like that, he's hopeless.' Brazil's third goal renews suspicions about the white referee, but it doesn't change the overall view. 'We're coming home but it isn't a problem. It's our first time in a World Cup and we've done well.' The party gets under way and invades the whole city. 'Because we're in Ghana and we're happy. Even if we don't win, it's OK just the same because we're in Ghana and we're happy.' The women had started singing this at the end of the first half, when Adriano's goal had made it clear how things were going end up. The same song over and over again. At the end of the game the streets of Chorkor fill up just the same: first women and children, then all the others. Processions, singing, dancing, horns hooting, whistles blowing, flags waving. 'What if they'd won?'

you think. It would probably have been just the same. What prevails is the desire to party, to celebrate, to be together and, in the case in point, to shout your anger at the *oblanie,* the white man who has once more tricked the black, this time dressed up as a Slovak referee.

After we have taken a few photos, Kofi says it is best to leave. He knows that the promenade will soon be packed with people and that it will be difficult to get past. Maybe he also knows that being here is no longer all that advisable for a white. He is right. If, in the street where the Appiah family live, I am seen as something of a hero, the rest of the neighbourhood does not share the affection. At the first red traffic light, I smile at the people in the car beside us but Kofi gets insulted because he is the white man's chauffeur and they insult me because I am white. A hand is raised to strike me, then another. Kofi swerves away and decides we are not going to stop at any more traffic lights until we get out of Chorkor. It is a turbulent, not exactly glorious exit – peaceful Ghana must have a more aggressive soul than I imagined. Once the storm is over, Kofi and his Triumph relax. He lets the motor cruise along, he sits back and, with a reassuring roar, we head away from the sea. Finally, I say goodbye to my saviour. Ghana haven't won, the miracle hasn't happened. But it does not matter 'because we are in Ghana and we're happy here'.

11. Nemo propheta in patria

In Africa one of the most common dreams – one of the easiest to achieve, within anyone's reach – is tied to sport. To the success that opens up the doors to Europe. Or America or Asia or even Africa itself. Today, in fact, you can emigrate to countries all over the continent where more money circulates than in your own. Football and athletics are the classic means of escape. Behind them in the league table of redemption and success through sport come boxing, basketball and rugby. It all depends on the country. Football is the only cross-border dream, the only sport synonymous with money, earnings and status in every country in Africa. Today about 3,000 African footballers play in championships outside their countries of origin. At every latitude and at every level: from the top divisions in Italy, Spain and England to the second division in China or amateur leagues in many European countries, and even in the championships of the Seychelles and Uganda. In all cases, they earn more than they would at home, so it is necessary to get up and go, to emigrate, to seek fortune elsewhere.

Nemo propheta in patria (no one is a prophet in his homeland) should be written on the passports of African footballers. The only leagues within the continent that can guarantee decent earnings are in South Africa, Tunisia, Egypt and Morocco. 'Foreigners' flock in from the rest of Africa, quality players to a man. Athletics is the second big dream, but only in recent years has it begun to expand. And to ruin itself, what with the Kenyans changing name and embracing the flags of wealthy Arab states such as Qatar, betraying their traditions and sometimes even their own fathers. Today Gregory Konchellah, the son of Billy, the 800 metres world champion in 1987 and 1991, is called Youssef Saad Kamel and runs for Bahrain.

Ethiopia, Kenya, Algeria and Morocco are famous for their long- and middle-distance runners; west Africa (Nigeria, Ghana, Cameroon) for its sprinters; South Africa for its marathon runners. Otherwise, every country has its own sporting schools: boxing in Ghana, rugby in South Africa, tennis in Morocco, basketball in Nigeria, a springboard for the United States.

The African sporting dream is born, grows and explodes in the streets. There are hardly any facilities but raw talent abounds. In Africa, even when sport reaps in money (in the event, for example, of qualification for the World Cup or sponsorships by multinational giants), this promptly ends up in the pockets of a few officials, never in investment for the general public. Officials complain loudly about the football exodus but they do nothing at all to develop their countries' sporting infrastructure. For economic and structural reasons, not even football giants such as Nigeria and Cameroon are capable of organising decent league tournaments. Since standards are high, everyone tries to go elsewhere and many succeed. It used to happen in the Eighties when players such as George Weah, Stephen Keshi, Rashidi Yekini and Abedi Pelé from Liberia, Nigeria and Ghana moved on to other African championships before heading for Europe. It still happens, the flow moving mostly in the direction of Tunisia, Morocco, Egypt and South Africa. Everyone is looking for a stroke of luck. If things go well, they travel to England, Spain or Italy; if they go badly even Malaysia or Vietnam will do.

African sportsmen are left to grow without a safety net, especially from the health point of view. In Africa they die of sport because there are no checks and until they come to Europe (though sometimes, as we have seen, that is not enough) congenital defects not seen as serious may cost lives. The other problem is that in Africa they dream of playing sport at the top level but they are always at risk of falling foul of unscrupulous agents and wheeler-dealers. This is why those 3,000 footballers may seem a multitude, but are in reality only a handful in proportion to the amount of talent available among Africa's over 600 million inhabitants. Oddly enough, there are still very few African agents. The dream requires a certain amount of assistance. Often the unresolved relationship stemming from the horrible 'master and servant' bond of colonial memory means that African athletes think they need whites to convert their talent into cash. The national-team manager has to be white, otherwise in many cases he is not listened to and respected, especially if he has not played in Europe and accumulated a fortune. The agent also has to be white, again out of respect, a respect the black struggles to win with European clubs.

If I had to make one criticism of African players outside Africa, it would be that they have not yet learned to give something back to the game at home. Now there are maybe two generations of African footballers who have been to Europe, winning, earning and playing at top level, and learning from the best coaches. Alas, no one seems ready yet to go home to spread all this wealth. When things go badly, some even give up immediately. In the case of a youngster of 16 who wants to come to Europe, would it not be better for him to be accompanied by a compatriot who has already trodden this sometimes painful path?

In Africa it sometimes seems that talent counts for nothing, and the concept could be extended to other fields of artistic application. Talents grow without great schools from which to learn, in facilities that, seen from Europe, fill one with anger or, viewed with a less partisan eye, with affection. There are no gymnasiums, no training equipment, no proper running tracks, no decent training centres. No nutritionists, no psychologists, no physiotherapists, no medical specialists. There are only great passion, a great desire and a love of sport, the universal dream of people who are still hungry.

One day Alhaji Grusa, president of King Faisal Babies, a small but well organised Ghanaian club (the one that produced Samuel Kuffour, who went on to be a Champions League winner with Bayern Munich), asked me to follow him to the suburbs of Accra to see a promising youth league match. It was a top-of-the-table clash between two teams based in the capital. I accepted willingly and with my faithful driver Dunia – beaming smile, almost toothless, eyes that move with a life of their own – at the wheel, we set off for the pitch. After half an hour or so, we stopped. Around us were dirt roads, low huts, general poverty, washing hanging out and a fountain that seemed to be the heart of the neighbourhood. Women and children came and went carrying buckets, canisters, bottles and other receptacles. There was also quite a large crowd standing in a rectangle. I worked out that the football pitch would be in the middle of them. I followed hot on the heels of Alhaji. The crowd stood back to let him pass. Their reverence and admiration was partly due to the fact that, if he is in a good mood, he is capable of pulling cedi notes from the sleeve of his blue *bubu* and handing them out. I managed to get a good spot.

We stood on the touchline. There were no stands but there must have been about a thousand onlookers. The touchlines and goal-lines were virtually marked by the spectators themselves. The other lines were dug out as opposed to chalked. It was a dirt pitch and the rain that had fallen in the days before the game had reshaped it. It sloped considerably from one wing to the other and running through the penalty area to my left was what in Europe would be defined as a stream. In arid regions such as this it was more like a river. Following the slope of the pitch, it cut across the field diagonally from the edge of the penalty area to the corner flag.

The left-winger who was playing on my side was very skilful. When he took on his man, he would calculate the distance from the stream and touch the ball just enough to nudge it over the water. Then, imitating the movement of the ball, he would jump over the outstretched legs of the defender and the stream. A superb piece of technique. There were puddles everywhere but the dry part of the field was as hard as iron. That did not stop the players from making 'African Cup-style tackles', a phrase coined by Gigi Buffon to describe a murderous lunge by the Ivorian Saliou Lassissi on Alen Boksic in a Lazio v Parma match a few years ago.

What struck me was the incredible level of skill. I could see why so many people had turned up to see the game. The players were very good. After about 20 minutes, the referee attracted my attention. He seemed very agitated. He looked at me, then started to gesticulate and talk. Not in English, but in Ga, the language of the Accra region. I was puzzled. Was he talking to me? I looked round and saw that the person he was talking to was standing right behind me. He was a middle-aged man feverishly unbuttoning his shirt as if he was about to get changed. He suddenly disappeared, swallowed up by the crowd. I watched him walk to a tree, sit down and complete the operation he had begun while talking to the ref. Another five minutes went by and he reappeared in a black strip with a linesman's flag in his hand. He pushed his way through the crowd and sprinted leftwards to the half he had to supervise. He made a brief sign to the ref and he was off. Though nobody had paid much attention or protested, there had only been one linesman before he took the field.

I could write a separate book about African referees. About their creativity, their incompetence, their absent-mindedness, their sloppiness. The best of the bunch, Said Belqola of Morocco, who refereed the World

Cup final in 1998, unfortunately died when he was only 45. The others muddle along and CAF seems to take pleasure in promoting incapable refs. A decisive Ivory Coast v Cameroon qualifying match for the World Cup in Germany was entrusted to the Tunisian Mourad Daami. Here are a couple of memorable moments in his career taken from an article I wrote during the 2000 African Cup of Nations:

> Kumasi, Ghana. The quarter-finals of the African Cup of Nations. The host team against South Africa. A well played, fair game. In the first half just one booking: Eric Tinkler of South Africa. At the start of the second half, Tinkler goes in hard on Kwame Ayew. The Tunisian referee Mourad Daami is about to book him again but he cannot find his yellow card. Daami starts to lose his cool. He searches in all his pockets, front, back, jersey, shorts. Nothing. He is now panicking. And he cannot remember whether Tinkler has already been booked. So he goes to the touchline and asks the fourth official for confirmation. 'He's already been booked,' they tell him. Daami goes back to the centre of the field and, since he can't find his yellow card, takes out his red one. He tries to explain to Tinkler that he is not being sent off directly but receiving a second booking.
>
> Lagos, Nigeria. The final of the African Cup of Nations. CAF has obviously admired the Tunisian referee Daami's comic skills and has decided to give him the final. Everything runs quite smoothly. This time he has all his cards in the right places, where they are easy to find. True, at a certain point the Nigerian Oliseh gets off with just a booking after retaliating to a foul and throwing a punch at Geremi of Cameroon. But Daami probably wants to save his party piece for the end. The match finishes 2-2. Extra time and penalties. Cameroon are leading 3-2, and Ikpeba goes to the spot for Nigeria. He shoots powerfully and hits the bar: the ball rebounds downwards, well over the line. Referee Daami does not hesitate for a moment. For him it is not a goal. He does not even consult the linesman who is perfectly positioned on the goal-line. He has no doubts. Cameroon have won the African Cup of Nations.

Here is another pearl from the same tournament.

> Charles Massembe of Uganda got up to all sorts in the semi-final between DR Congo and South Africa. He booked the Congolese centre-forward Tondelua twice without sending him off. He produced nine minutes' injury time before extra time. Towards the end of the second half of extra time, there was a clear penalty for South Africa but he turned it into a free-kick on the edge of the box. In Burkina, I once saw a team play with 12 men for a whole minute before the referee allowed the substitution...

In 2005 Gambia surprisingly qualified for the Under-17 World Cup in Peru. Three African teams were allowed in the competition, the top three from the continental championship. Gambia excelled themselves and actually won the tournament they had organised. In the final it was not easy to get the better of Ghana, who had beaten them in the preliminary rounds.

On May 22 in Banjul the match was stuck at 0-0. The ground was packed and there was a big-time atmosphere for the country famous for its beaches and for its hardly flattering nickname: the suppository of Africa, on account of its geographical position, an enclave surrounded by Senegal. The crowd wanted victory and the cup, as did the politicians. And victory promptly arrived. Three minutes from the end of the game, Ousmane Jallow beat the Ghana keeper Seth Obodai. But poor Obodai had been distracted by a fan who had sneaked onto the field and appeared in the penalty area at the decisive moment. Like a piece of improvised street theatre, he had attracted Obodai's attention and allowed Jallow to score. The Ghanaians protested and the crowd reacted angrily, pelting them with stones and anything else they could find on the terraces. The Lesotho referee Paul Phomane allowed the goal to stand and Gambia thus won its first historic football prize. CAF punished the Gambian football federation for its fans' unruliness with a $10,000 fine, later reduced to $5,000 – case closed. It may only have been an Under-17 Championship, but it was a final.

It is hard to stay on and play in Africa for many reasons. Not for the refereeing, of course, but for all the rest. Where does the money go to that pours in from CAF and FIFA? Every year FIFA in Zurich gives CAF in Cairo $2.5 million, and every African federation then cashes a cheque of $250,000 from FIFA. Since 1998 Liberia has received $6.2 million from FIFA to create football facilities, a grant sanctioned by the world federation's 'Goal' development project, a programme from which many other African federations have benefited. In Liberia, a country where running water and electricity are lacking, you can do many of things with $6.2 million. A few months after the donation, Sepp Blatter turned up in Monrovia for the inauguration of the training centre that had been built with the money – a synthetic grass pitch without floodlights. The Liberian championship struggles along, stopping and starting amid a thousand difficulties. Few teams, poor standards, no facilities, no money. George Weah always looked after the national team on his own. Then even he got fed up.

Some stories could only come out of Africa. Or so it seems. Stories whose plots develop against a background of war, disease and poverty. Stories of passion, solidarity and spirit of initiative. Liberia has been torn apart by civil war for 13 years. More than 400,000 people have been killed and millions of others forced to abandon their homes, sometimes their country. In Ghana there are 42,000 Liberian refugees. The conflict exploded again in all its brutality a couple of weeks ago. On June 4 the news that president Charles Taylor had been accused by the international tribunal of war crimes, in the conflict that has just come to an end in neighbouring Sierra Leone, immediately unleashed an offensive by his opponents. The rebels got as far as the gates of Monrovia before being repelled. Over 400 people died and 60,000 were evacuated. On Tuesday the parties met in Accra and signed an armistice based on an agreement whereby Taylor would relinquish power before the end of the month. On Friday, however, the president backtracked, suggesting he will stand again for election at the end of his mandate in 2004. The country has thus been thrown into chaos once more.

This is why football is not a priority in Liberia at the moment. Maybe it has never been a priority. But the fact the country produced George Weah – in 1995 the first non-European to be named European Footballer of the Year – ensured that the flame of football, albeit feeble among the fires that were flaring all over the country, would stay alive. Last March the Minister of Sport Max Dennis decided to dismantle the national team, but the president of the football federation Edwin Snowe opposed the move. 'We'll go ahead at any price,' he said. But playing football costs money. Fed up with having to subsidise the team out of their own pockets, the famous names of Liberian football – Weah, his cousin James Debbah, Zizi Roberts, Sebwe and Makor – have all abandoned the Lone Star. On March 30 last year, the victory over Ethiopia ignited enthusiasm yet again. After all, just two years ago Liberia were in the African Cup of Nations and fought it out with Nigeria to the last breath to qualify for the 2002 World Cup.

Yesterday in Monrovia, Liberia had to play Guinea in a qualifying match for the next African Cup of Nations in Tunisia in 2004. CAF decided to shift the match to Accra for security reasons. The Ghanaian capital is not far away, yet the federation failed to produce the €10,000 needed to pay for the flight. On Friday enthusiasm was further checked when Ghana Airways decided to refuse the Liberian federation's umpteenth IOU. It was June 20, by an odd stroke of fate World Refugees Day. In Liberia they had a brainwave. The refugees in Ghana could take the field against Guinea. The Liberians who had to flee a country in flames have been living in a camp in Buduburam, 25 miles west of Accra, for over ten years.

Today the camp hosts 30,000 refugees in all, mostly Liberians. In the course of time, amid violence, strife and intermittent humanitarian aid, restaurants, bars and even an internet cafe have sprung up in Buduburam. People try to get by as best they can and this being Africa, where football is part of life, on May 3, Shoes FC beat FC Professional 2-1 in the final of the impromptu refugee camp championship. Inevitably enough the local hero, Francis Doe, was christened the new Weah. When the news of the upcoming Guinea match spread in Buduburam, enthusiasm shot soared. 'We'll make life tough for the Guineans. Our prestige is at stake,' announced OP Myers, captain of the refugee camp national team.

In Monrovia feverish attempts were underway to get the real national team onto the plane for Accra. As always everyone's thoughts turned to George Weah. The former AC Milan player, 37 in October, retired from national team in January 2002 after the defeat against Nigeria in the African Cup of Nations, but this year he played again for Al Jazira in the United Arab Emirates. Weah has maintained the team virtually single-handedly for years, paying for travel, food, accommodation, jerseys and boots. He was captain and trainer and, when necessary, he used to play deep as a sweeper. After failing to reach the World Cup finals and being ignominiously knocked out of the African Cup of Nations, he gave up. But the heart has its reasons and on Friday Weah, in New York, tried to solve the matter by offering to come up with the $12,000 required. When the agreement fell through with Ghana Airways, he found another company, Wheshua Airlines, that was prepared to carry his former team-mates to Accra. Wheshua Airlines, alas, does not have a licence to land in Ghana.

So it was the refugees who eventually took the field. Seven players were making their debut in the match of their lives, supported by thousands of fans who had come to Accra's Olympic Stadium from the camp in Buduburam and by four pros: Daye, formerly of Bastia now of Club Africain of Tunis, Seator of Esperance of Tunis, Kieh, who plays in Cyprus, and Lomell of Maritzburg in the South African second division. Also from South Africa came Kojo but a bout of malaria prevented him from taking the field. Guinea turned out their first-choice side made up mainly of professionals playing in Europe. Group Two was very open with four teams divided by only six points but only the group winner qualifying. After just 11 minutes, Souleymane Youla, with 11 goals this year for Genclerbirligi, a surprise third in the Turkish league, gave Guinea the lead with a well taken free-kick from the edge of the box. Miraculously, the Liberia captain Prince Daye managed to equalise nine minutes later with a long-range left-foot volley. As the minutes passed, Liberia dropped back to protect a struggling defence. A draw would have left the team with hopes intact for the last game against Niger but in the fifth minute of the second half a defensive mistake let through Youla, who dribbled past the goalkeeper Glasgow to score. It was the end of the road for the Lone Star.

The refugees could not stand the pace. They were never dangerous in the second half and the match lost its edge. For Liberia it was virtually farewell to the African Cup of Nations. On June 6 they played their last match against Niger at N'Djamey. Again away from home but with no Liberian refugee camp to count upon. The Lone Star seemed loner than ever.

Gazzetta dello Sport, June 22, 2003

Cameroon and Nigeria, to cite two countries that pocket a lot of money and do not spend any of it on the game, have received millions of dollars from Puma and Nike for shirt sponsorship. In 2004 Togo banked a cheque for $600,000 from Puma. Qualifying for the World Cup in Asia in 2002 and playing three matches there yielded €3.5 million to five African federations: Cameroon, Nigeria, South Africa, Tunisia and Senegal (who, as quarter-finalists, received much more). The Indomitable Lions reached the knockout stages of four consecutive World Cups from 1990 to 2002. But the national championship is ridiculous, especially in relation to the high standards of Cameroonian players. Insofar as they handle far too much money to be left to their fate, the football federations of the African countries are closely connected to the Ministry of Sport. But the money in question is never reinvested in football.

It is not rare for footballers who play in Europe to pay for their own air fares when they are called up for their national teams – and then struggle to be refunded. A few years ago, out of love for his country, the Manchester City and Zimbabwe centre-forward Benjani Mwaruwari, who was playing for Auxerre, paid for a fortnight's stay in France for the whole national side, a delegation of 40 people, to train properly for a vital African Cup of Nations match against Rwanda. The federation only had to pay for the air fares and most of the players called up were living in Europe anyway.

Squabbles over bonuses are a regular occurrence, with players wasting time and energy pinning down agreements that are invariably disregarded by federations. Hence the poor showings at World Cups when minds are occupied more by tiresome union battles than the thought of competition. That was the case with Cameroon in 1994 and 1998, and Nigeria in 1998 and 2002. And here is another paradox: before Ivory Coast v Cameroon, a decisive qualifying match for the World Cup in Germany, Samuel Eto'o promised the whole national team, 22 players plus training staff including the Portuguese manager Artur Jorge, a bonus of $2,000 each in the event of victory. Cameroon won 3-2, and Eto'o had to fork out over $60,000. Again out of love for his country.

It is impossible to know where football money from Europe to Africa goes to but the situation is not dissimilar to that of other interventions and aid in the same countries. Since widespread political instability means that it is impossible to know what will happen tomorrow, people who occupy positions of power in Africa tend to seek immediate profit. They never plan ahead with long-term productive investment and development projects. Viewing things from grassroots level, it is thus better to go and earn your living elsewhere. In Barcelona, like Eto'o, or with St Michel United in the Seychelles, like the Kenyan Moses Gikenyi.

Journeys of hope. From Africa to Europe. From countries destroyed by civil war towards a reality that is bound to be better than the one left behind. Tragic, uncertain voyages in buckets that, seen from this side of Mediterranean, do not even look as if they could float. Abdullahi Dahir Ali and Collins John do not know each other. They are both African, they are both footballers (strikers to be precise) and they both tried to come to Europe by boat. But there the similarities end. The first, a Somali, didn't even manage to embark. The second, a Liberian, today plays for Leicester City on loan from Fulham and he was once on the fringe of the Dutch national team. For him things have worked out well.

There is a lot of talk these days about illegal immigrants, often from Libya, disembarking on Italian shores. That is what Ali tried to do, but he was unlucky. 'I'm 28, I'm married, I've got two children and in Somalia I was a footballer. I played as a striker for Banadir Telecom and the national team.' After a *coup d'état* overthrew Siad Barre's socialist government in 1991, the former Italian colony was thrown into chaos and anarchy. The northern part of the country broke away and claimed independence. The transition government appointed in 2000 failed to improve the situation. The Somali national team rarely plays and since 1991 it has only ever played abroad. After ten years or so of suspensions and fitful resumptions, the championship groaned back into action in 2006. At the moment there are 11 teams.

'I thought that things might improve, but I ended up losing all hope, and in August 2002 I decided to leave for Europe,' Ali said. 'I took a bus from Mogadishu to Galka'yo, 600 kilometres to the north. From there I reached Addis Ababa, the capital of Ethiopia, where I gathered some money from relatives and met some other young Somali men who were looking for a way to get to Italy, via Libya. We all set off without documents. The first stage of the journey was through Sudan: we crossed the border on foot, through a forest. We were all frightened. Then we travelled on to the capital, Khartoum, where there are Somalis who organise the trip to Libya by off-road vehicle. Once in Tripoli, again thanks to a group of compatriots, I came into contact with the organisation that arranges the last part of the journey. I paid an advance of $1,000 for the crossing to Italy. All the people who have paid are brought together in a big shed where they wait to depart. They'd told me to be wary of the inhabitants of the neighbourhood, who are always ready to report any suspicious movements, but I was out of luck. Three times I had to escape from the hut, and in the last round-up I was arrested by the Libyan police. After a few days in prison, they put me on a plane to Somalia. This happened last August. Two years after leaving, I was back in Mogadishu. But I'm not giving up. I want to try again, life's too bad here. I want to live better and study and maybe play football.'

Collins John left Monrovia, the capital of Liberia, in 1994. He was eight years old; two years earlier the civil war that had split the country had killed his father. His mother woke him up and told him not to make a noise. The moment had come: with his two brothers and sister, all younger than him, Collins was setting off for Rotterdam. A long, difficult journey. But all went well. The Liberian family arrived safe and sound and asked for political asylum. For two years the Johns were held in a reception camp; then, at last, things began to move. After being transferred to the town of Nijverdal, they were given Dutch documents and life began anew. Collins John started playing football again. No longer in the dusty streets of Monrovia but now on the grass fields of the Netherlands. His father was also a good player but he had never had the chance to be spotted. His son was more fortunate. He signed for FC Twente and, in a flash, at the age of just 16, found himself in the first team. It was the summer of 2002, precisely when Ali was beginning his incredible journey from Somalia to Italy. When Collins John scored he would pull up his jersey to reveal the message 'To My Father' on his vest underneath.

After a season and a half with Twente, where he scored 11 goals in 35 matches, he moved to Fulham in the Premier League. Here too every goal was followed by a dedication, 'For My Past', Collins's way of bringing to an end a long period of suffering and uncertainty. His Dutch passport got John into the country's various youth teams, and in August 2004 Marco van Basten called him up for a friendly against Sweden. John was not selected but he already thought he was on a par with Van Nistelrooy and co. Collins John was 22 on October 17, 2007 and his brothers, 13 and 16 respectively, are now also on FC Twente's books. 'My heart and my blood are still Liberian but I could only return to my country if things improved. Holland has treated us well. It's no coincidence that, though I admire George Weah, my idol is Patrick Kluivert.' Abdullahi Dahir Ali's idol is the trafficker in people who tries somehow to cross the Mediterranean in a small boat. After pocketing $1,000.

12. Italians in Africa

'**H**ello, who's speaking?'
   'It's Bomber, what are you doing?'
   I thought I was going to faint with laughter. I was in a hotel in Johannesburg, working. The call arrived late in the morning. It was Roberto Pruzzo, 'Bomber' as he was known to AS Roma supporters in the Eighties – and evidently even to himself. He had also been *O Rei di Crocefieschi* (the King of Crocefieschi), the Ligurian village where he was born, to Genoa supporters in the Seventies. He was at the African Cup of Nations on behalf of AS Roma. That morning he was bored and looking for company. Africa scared him to death (he was frightened of the lizards in particular) but always ready to laugh about his fear. He'd been cross at being met at the airport by a girl – a Lazio supporter at that – who did not know him. She had a card with his name on it written in felt-tip pen. 'Pruzzo', it said, not even 'Bomber'.

I've started with Pruzzo because, after all these years, the episode is still very fresh in my memory. And because, in 1996 in South Africa, I came into close contact for the first time with the many Italians who had decided to follow the African Cup of Nations.

The Italian interest in Africa had blossomed in 1992 in Senegal. Legend has it that, in Dakar, Arrigo Sacchi was desperately in need of a *tisane*, a herbal tea popular in Italy. He started swearing because he could not find one anywhere. Italians abroad are a subject for study, for leg-pulling, for sociological essays. African footballing missions in particular provide interesting material for behavioural analysis. There are various categories of Italian football travellers in Africa, some of whom shift from one category to another depending on geographical area, mood and familiarity with places and people.

There are the sex tourists for whom Africa is one big brothel. Then there are more easy-going types for whom Africa is a wonderful place

– but they would prefer to be back home on Lake Como. There are the enthusiasts, who have always had the *mal d'Afrique* inside without realising it. There are the versatile, who feel somewhat uneasy but lap up the experience. There are the professionals, who go where you tell them – Africa, Norway, China, wherever. There are paranoids, who say 'damn the club president who sent me here'. There are the shy, who begin gradually and end up falling in love with the place. There are the curious, who ask lots of questions. And there are the presumptuous, who assume they know everything.

So many stories to tell: the Roman youngsters who won the tender for the accreditation and ticket printing system for the African Cup of Nations in Burkina Faso; Antonio Matarrese, now president of the Italian league, who played tennis with Roger Milla in Ouagadougou and beat him; the Roman photographer who liked the African Cup of Nations so much he took his girlfriend there and stayed on holiday in the countries in which he worked; the journalist-anthropologist from Turin who stayed not in a hotel but at the home of *Burkinabé* friends whom he had met God knows where in order to improve his degree thesis. Africa strips naked, bares and X-rays the moods and passions of all those who approach her. It is hard to hide there. In more than ten years' travelling round the continent, I've witnessed many stories of Italians on holiday. Most of them amusing.

'Voulez vous tromber? Avec moi!' The offer came from the taxi next to mine. It was shouted out in the Tunisian night by a Udinese scout. The French was so-so – he meant to say *coucher* – but the sexual innuendo was understood perfectly. The scene was so surreal that even our taxi driver laughed. He spoke no Italian but he understood that hybrid French perfectly, partly because it was accompanied by mimicry that would have left Marcel Marceau unimpressed but in no doubt about the meaning.

This was in 1994. Four years later Udinese decided to change their scout for Africa. The new man, Gianni Dini, had pale, glazed-over eyes and white hair. He was a great smoker and had a thick Roman accent in which he swore a lot but he was a lovely man. He fell in love with Africa immediately and his passion has never waned. He not only did the official rounds – African Cups of Nations and major tournaments – but also embarked on extreme scouting expeditions among the minor leagues. His passion was overpowering. He would leave Rome with his suitcase full and come home with it empty. He gave away as much as he could to anyone who asked. He was a great travelling companion. Quiet but ever-ready to explode, he defined himself as an 'ex-anarchist'. It was hard to understand what had attracted him to football. He threw himself into Africa so much that he tended to forget that some situations can prove dangerous.

In 1999 I set off with Dini for the Under-20 World Cup in Nigeria. After a few days in Lagos we travelled out to Kaduna. One morning he wanted to go to see a match in Kano, five hours away by car. I was unconvinced and decided not to go with him. At one in the morning he was still not back. Yet his match had finished at seven o'clock the night before. I waited up for him like a worried parent. The hours ticked by... two o'clock, three o'clock. Without a mobile phone, all I could do was wait. When I saw Dini appear at last, in the hall of the Hamdala Hotel, I thought I was seeing a ghost. He was goggle-eyed with fear. I can still see his terror-stricken expression clearly in front of me. He hugged me: 'Filì, you can't believe what hell I've been through!' The road home was a straight line cut through the forest that was controlled by gangs waiting for an opportunity to make a bit of money. The road was dotted with makeshift roadblocks, knocked together with bits of burned wood, overturned oil drums and miscellaneous other obstacles, one after another. Dini's driver had stopped at the first but the experience had been so daunting he had decided to drive straight through the others. If there was enough room on the sides of the road, he would drive round them, otherwise he would ram through them. Dini had realised that if the driver was frightened then there really was cause to worry. The journey had turned into an ordeal and had lasted an eternity.

Gianni was one of the leading players in the celebrated Eau Vive revolt in Burkina Faso. That time his revolutionary spirit was inflamed for other reasons. As mentioned in Chapter 2, the Eau Vive was a French restaurant run by nuns, one of a chain to be found all over the world, even in downtown Rome. It was an unusual place: a garden full of flowers, nice atmosphere, good food, medium-high prices. In Ouagadougou for the African Cup of Nations it became the dinnertime haunt for the packed group of Italians – journalists, scouts, agents – in town for the tournament. We used to meet there every night and there were always more than ten of us round the table.

'Filì, go to the nuns in the kitchen and tell them how to cook this. *Al dente*, mind. I trust them for the sauce.' The former Lazio, Juventus and Roma star Lionello Manfredonia was handing me a kilo pack of spaghetti. The morning before, arriving in Ouagadougou, all his possessions had been stolen. For a day and a half poor Lionello had dashed around in a state of seething anger from one run-down police station to another, making statements to policemen who worked in slow motion. But he told the story with humour, almost with a smile – even laughter when he came to the most surreal parts. Then, as if by magic, the stolen goods had reappeared. They included the pack of spaghetti. I took it to the nuns in the kitchen and gave them the instructions as explained to me by Lionello, who was in Ouaga working for Parma.

On the third or fourth evening at the Eau Vive an incident occurred. The bill, which had been increasing gradually over the previous days, had shot up by a disproportionate amount. It was obviously my job to complain to the nun at the cash desk. But I was not alone. Speaking in a Frenchified Italian of broken words, random stresses and sounds that ended suddenly with an accented 'e', others had rebelled too. They were led by Serie A scouts Silvano Flaborea and Franco Janich, the latter a former Italy international. The nun tried to argue but her case was flimsy. Then Gianni Dini, who had so far remained silent, got up. In his Italian peppered with Roman dialect, Gianni delivered a speech to the nun. What he said basically was that he came from a country of priests and he had never liked them. It was unthinkable for him to have to come to Africa and have the piss taken out of him by a bunch of nuns. He was an anarchist, for crying out loud. The bill was immediately reduced. The day after was my birthday. When I got out of my taxi, I found 20 or so nuns lined up on either side of the entrance singing *Happy Birthday*. An impromptu chorus but an effective one. At the end of the evening, a large cake with candles was brought out, on the house. The incident of the day before forgotten – the Eau Vive revolt had succeeded.

I had met Manfredonia two years earlier in South Africa, when 'Bomber' Pruzzo was also there. That time I helped to organise the journey for the packed platoon of Italian observers. That meant many a headache on account of their absurd demands. All this was worsened by the fact that they were all expecting to find a sort of African Switzerland, whereas the country was actually in a state of general confusion and hardly anything worked. At the Holiday Inn in Milpark, the university area of Johannesburg, the telephone alarms in the rooms, programmed automatically by the switchboard and apparently unstoppable, went off every morning at five o'clock. The arguments the incensed Italians had with the small, rotund receptionist Salamina (her name was printed on a badge on her blazer) had become the stuff of pure comedy. Maybe it was the fault of their pidgin English, maybe it was Salamina's laid-back approach to her job, but the fact is that the alarms kept on ringing at five in the morning for the duration of our stay. The bags under our eyes grew in size.

Lionello was moved by the African Cup of Nations opening ceremony – an overdose of music, emotion, sound, sensation, colour and dancing – at Soccer City, the stadium near Soweto. He wasn't the only one. The Italians present were not exactly *au fait* with reggae, dub and ambient music but they all allowed themselves to be drowned by that musical tsunami. Two hours of all-out partying was closed by a speech from Nelson Mandela. The Italians did not understand the literal meaning of the words but they grasped their sense perfectly. Charisma knows no lexical boundaries: it always works. On the way home, standing on the corner waiting for our minibus to arrive, Manfredonia, characteristically dry and articulate, had amused the audience with the story of his adventure as a 'spectator' at the 1978 World Cup, where he was an unused squad member. 'Listen, boss,' he told Enzo Bearzot in a private conversation, 'if I have to go somewhere on holiday I prefer to choose the destination myself. OK?' The Italy manager did not turn a hair and the Lazio defender's international career virtually ended there. 'Just think what a fool I was,' laughed Manfredonia.

The Tuscan coach Nedo Sonetti was also in South Africa in 1996. He was unemployed at the time and had decided to go for a professional refresher trip. In the hotel before the semi-final between South Africa and Ghana he had met Abedi Pelé, a former protégé of his at Torino. The Ghanaian had given him a good grandstand ticket for the game, a rare commodity in those days of heady pro-*Bafana* mania. Pruzzo had to make do with a ticket on the terraces. But once they reached the ground Sonetti tore up his precious ticket and accompanied Bomber on his excursion among the local fans. The two were worried at first but ended up having a rare old time.

'I'd bought myself a cap in the South African colours with *Bafana Bafana* written on it,' recalls Pruzzo. 'I was worried because I was sitting beside a guy who seemed unreal. Before the game he was completely still as if he was praying. I didn't have time to tell Nedo and when the match kicked off my neighbour underwent a total transformation. He was very tense and he leaned on me as he watched the game unfold. He was sitting on my left and since South Africa were attacking to our right it felt as if he was pushing the team forward against my shoulder. I would occasionally offer him a cigarette but he seemed to be in a trance. At one point a fan appeared stripped to the waist. He seemed a bit soft in the head. I thought he'd fallen down from the tier above. He went up to a policeman and started shadow-boxing.'

'We had to do the Mexican wave,' says Sonetti. 'We both joined in, and we really enjoyed ourselves. We were the only whites there and at a certain point they realised we weren't South Africans. When we told them we were Italians, they made a big fuss of us.' 'It's great to remember that South African experience,' says Pruzzo. 'In fact we'll never forget it.'

If scouts and the like spend only a few days or weeks at a time in Africa, coaches stay much longer. There have never been many Italian coaches in Africa: Eugenio 'Iron Sergeant' Bersellini, whose experience in Libya I followed a little; Romano Mattè in Mali, another adventure that I did not experience first hand; and former World Cup winner Marco Tardelli in Egypt for a brief spell as national coach. Then there were Beppe Dossena in Ghana and Franco Scoglio in Tunisia. I spent a lot of time in Africa with the last two, sharing their passions, difficulties, enthusiasms and defeats. Dossena and Scoglio stumbled in to Africa in different ways. When I began to write this book Scoglio, 'The Professor', was still alive. Today he is no longer with us, having died on live TV in his adopted city of Genoa. The memory of his African experience thus takes on a new form, no longer a repeatable success story – Scoglio had received plenty of offers from Africa – but a closed chapter. But what an important chapter it was. When Scoglio arrived in Tunisia, in August 1998, he was breaking away from Italian football, disappointed by his umpteenth dismissal at Torino, which he deemed totally unjustified. He had sent his CV to the Tunisian federation with references from FIFA and UEFA vice-president Antonio Matarrese, who had several friends in Africa. He was taken on and threw himself into the new experience with great zeal and enthusiasm. I went to see him almost immediately and he asked me to attend a national team training session at the Annexe, a pitch next to the El Menzah stadium in Tunis. Scoglio spoke neither French nor Arabic but he made himself understood and he captured the attention of his players, previously accustomed to the silence and brusque manners of the French-Polish coach Henryk Kasperczak.

'*Porte lu balon*,' he used to tell Khaled Badra, the sweeper in his strange mixture of Italian dialect and French. The Professor wanted to teach him to construct from the back, to come out of his area with the ball at his feet. I smiled, but Badra did exactly what he was told. 'He's better than Desailly,' said Scoglio. He was not being provocative; he believed in Badra because he believed in Tunisian football, in the talent of its young players and the standard of the game in general. Tunisia went on to win the African Cup of Nations in 2004, albeit with a different manager. Under Scoglio, two years earlier in Ghana, they were knocked out in the semi-final by a very strong Cameroon side who went on to become champions. Scoglio did not take it badly. He was happy and laid-back, perfectly at ease in the tournament.

His press conferences were great fun. At that point he was getting along famously with the French and I used to give him a hand with the English. He would get worked up and start explaining his tactics and arguing with the journalists just as he used to do on Italian television, with his usual sulking expression and attitude, but also with the same earnestness and good humour. The attention he devoted to them delighted the African journalists, who were used to being patronised by European coaches. They always had to drag away the Professor, otherwise he would have talked for hours.

He felt as if he was on a mission and the fact was much appreciated. He had practically taken Tunisia into the final stages of the World Cup when he received a call from Genoa in 2001. Scoglio was in a quandary. First he said yes, then he said no. He tried to hold onto both jobs, but the Tunisians were opposed to the idea. So Scoglio returned to Italy and saved Genoa

from relegation to Serie C1. Then he signed five of his Tunisian internationals, not out of personal interest but because he believed in them
and their ability. Things worked out badly for all concerned but that is of
little consequence. Scoglio remained very tied to Africa and to Tunisia.
He rented a house in Tunis and he left a very good impression all over
the country. 'A true friend of Tunisia', was how his former employers
at the Tunisian federation described him after his death. The acknowl-
edgment may sound banal, but it wasn't. It came from the heart because,
in Tunisia, Scoglio had coached with his heart.

Another Italian, Beppe Dossena, found a job in Africa in the summer
of 1998. In Italy he achieved little as a manager but that counts only up
to a certain point in Africa. What does count is the desire to put yourself
on the line. To change things by allowing yourself to be changed by
the environment. To impose your own ideas while listening to those
of others. To join in and let yourself be won over by a reality different
from your own. It is a reality that is at once slower and less developed
– football-wise and in every other sense – but also rich and bubbling
with enthusiasm. Dossena grasped all this and gave the impression he
felt more at home in Accra than in Bologna. When I used to meet him in
Ghana, it was as if he had undergone a physical mutation. His expression
was relaxed and his blue eyes used to open wide and shine, as if they were
continuously taking in something new, unusual, out of the ordinary.
This sort of transformation happens only rarely among Europeans and
I have learned to spot it. The Ghanaians were fond of Dossena who, in
view of his kindness and openness, they dubbed *coachito*. You could tell
he was fond of Ghana. 'I don't feel happy here,' he once said at a training
camp before a friendly against Holland in Arnhem. 'I need to return to
Africa.' He was joking – but only up to a point.

On the field things went reasonably well, but they could have gone better.
Victory at home in the African Under-20 Cup of Nations was followed by
an unlucky elimination on penalties in the Under-20 World Cup quarter-
finals in Nigeria against Spain, who went on to win the trophy. There
were a few good performances with the senior side, including a record
3-0 win against Cameroon and a defeat against South Africa at Kumasi
in the quarter-finals of the African Cup of Nations organised in 2000
by Ghana and Nigeria. The minimum objective had been the final, so
Dossena's dismissal at that point was automatic.

13. White magic

In Europe, some rely on holy water, like former Italy manager Giovanni Trapattoni, who put the stuff in his suitcase and took it to Asia with him for the 2002 World Cup. Some scatter salt in the goalmouth, some refuse to wear a certain numbered jersey, some cross themselves after scoring a goal or when they take the field, simply because that is what they used to do at Sunday school or what their mothers told them to. There are others who kiss rings and medallions and holy effigies of every shape and form.

Superstition, it's called. Nothing serious, just innocent rituals that have nothing magical about them, nothing tribal, nothing fetishistic. They are a link in the chain that goes from dressing room to pitch – players put on their shirts and their shorts and their shin pads, they lace up their boots (left first or right first but never random). Then there are the psychologists who, in some cases, become healers, hypnotists, gurus. Ruud Gullit and Marco van Basten turned to them, as did Glenn Hoddle and Steve McClaren. Even Nils Liedholm, the former AC Milan and Sweden international and manager of the AS Roma team that won the *Scudetto* in 1983, used to consult a soothsayer.

In Africa things are supposed to be different. After all, is Africa not the continent of black magic and witch doctors and voodoo? None of the African footballers ever speak openly about magic. But if you ask, they all have an anecdote to tell. The fact is that in Africa the relationship with the supernatural is strong. Mix it all together with religion, football, superstition and popular tradition and you get the magic potion that makes Africans footballers behave in a way that is bizarre, to say the least. In Europe that kind of behaviour takes on even more spectacular forms and values. Whether it produces results has yet to be demonstrated but since, once in a while, it apparently does – meaning that the witch doctor or *feticheur* or *muti*-man does his job well – so the tradition stays alive and perpetuates itself. This is why, in Europe, we continue to think of Africa as the continent of magic in all walks of life, football included. So we forget about Trapattoni's holy water at the World Cup. In 2002, not in 1950.

In the same year before Trap ran out of his precious liquid without managing to get his team to score a second precious goal against Korea or keep referee Byron Moreno in check, a diplomatic incident had almost occurred in Mali. The African Cup of Nations semi-final between Cameroon and Mali is about to take place at the 26 March Stadium in Bamako, the capital of Mali. The hosts are playing the reigning champions, the hot favourites. The atmosphere is highly charged. Early in the morning the stadium is already packed to capacity. In the eyes of the fans in the grandstand, who have been waiting for hours for the big event, even a simple pitch inspection can have the most unexpected consequences. It can be a pretext, an opportunity to jump to conclusions and start fighting. Winfried Schafer, Cameroon's German coach, and his assistant Thomas Nkono, the country's unforgettable goalkeeper in the World Cup in Spain in 1982, enter the ground and go out to check the pitch. It is stifling hot and the pitches for the African Cup of Nations in Mali haven't been exactly impeccable. It all happens in an instant. The crowd wakes up from the torpor brought on by the heat and cheap alcohol and begins first to bay, then to roar. All of a sudden Nkono is surrounded by the Mali military (it is a habit in Africa to use the infantry and even the cavalry at football matches). He is jostled to the ground, handcuffed and marched away amid the taunts of the ecstatic crowd. Schafer is not handcuffed – the white man always receives more respect – but he too is manhandled and taken away.

The charge? Nkono and his white assistant (in this case the roles are reversed because it's African 'business') are accused of sneakily trying to leave a magical charm on the field. The crooks are caught red-handed. At the stadium of course are the top brass of CAF for whom the Cup of Nations is a showcase. Seen live on television worldwide, the incident is a bad advertisement for African football. The bigwigs immediately dash down to the press room, where Nkono appears in handcuffs, surrounded by a bunch of soldiers. Schafer has already been released, but back on the field more scuffles break out between the Cameroon players and the zealous Malian infantrymen who have received strict orders to prevent the Indomitable Lions testing and inspecting the conditions of the patchy March 26 Stadium pitch. The chaos is total. Then the match starts, Cameroon win 3-0, Nkono is released and the President of the Republic of Mali, Alpha Oumar Konaré, goes to the guests' dressing room to apologise to Nkono on behalf of the nation. A diplomatic incident is avoided and the case is closed.

Putting objects in your own or the opponents' net on the advice of the *marabout* (a spiritual leader in Muslim areas of west Africa) is one of the most common practices and often has unsavoury consequences. Pedro Pablo Pasculli was a centre-forward from Argentina. Profiting from the reflected light generously cast by Diego Maradona, he played a few good seasons in Italy for Lecce. Subsequently, in May 2003, he somehow ended up as coach of Uganda where he stayed for a month, leading the Cranes in only one game – a decisive African Cup of Nations qualifier against Rwanda in Kampala. Uganda had not qualified since 1978, Rwanda had never done so. After a few minutes the Rwanda goalkeeper, Muhamud Mossi, stuck something to the net and set it on fire.

A length of string? A scrap of material? A bottle top? No one knew exactly what the object was but there were no doubts as to what it was for. It was a *muti*, a *juju*, a *honjon*. In other words, a highly potent amulet. The Uganda players all demanded that the Ethiopian linesman Lema Mesfin remove the object from the Rwanda net but the poor man was in an awkward position. Scared stiff, he refused to budge from the touchline. Maybe he too was under the power of the amulet. Then the Cranes went on the attack. If they were to have any chance of victory, they had to seize the object from Mossi's goal at all costs. The goal-line became a Maginot line. In the pitched battle that ensued, the Ugandans prevailed. The precious amulet was grabbed from the net and one of Pasculli's team raced off with it. As he sprinted away he was followed by a human snake: team-mates, opponents, policemen, the referee and the linesmen, totally unprepared to deal with such an unusual incident. Rwanda then hit back on the counter attack and managed to recover the booty. At that point, without any apparent logic, tempers calmed. After long arguments, the match then resumed.

Ten minutes or so later, the keeper made a second attempt to set the object on fire. And pandemonium broke out again. A repeat of the same scenes: like a brawl in a silent movie, kicking and punching, the referee losing control and the stadium going crazy. Then calm was restored. The amulet vanished for good but Rwanda won 1-0 to reach their first African Cup of Nations. 'In years and years of football, I've never seen anything like it,' was the shocked Pasculli's predictable comment. 'In South America there's no shortage of colourful incidents, but this was just too much. It's not football, it's magic, war, indiscipline.' Recently Pasculli was asked to take on the Uganda job again. The Argentine politely declined.

Try telling the Senegalese that such matters are not important. Senegal is an *avant garde* country in terms of the interaction between magic and tactics. In the golden years of Bruno Metsu, when the country reached the last eight of the Cup of Nations in 2000 and the final in 2002, before going on to the quarter-finals of the World Cup in Japan-Korea in the same year, many people were convinced the results were more due to the excellent *marabout* hired by the federation than to the football knowhow of the French coach who looked like a rock star. Who can say they were wrong?

In the 2000 Cup of Nations quarter-final against Nigeria in Lagos, Senegal surprisingly took the lead with a goal by Khalilou Fadiga, holding on until a quarter of an hour from the end. The Surulere stadium was a boiling cauldron. No one believed that Nigeria could lose at home against Senegal but Nwankwo Kanu, Taribo West and co seemed mesmerised. Then a Nigerian federation official decided to intervene. Kashimayo Laloko is a man of great experience in both the natural (he runs a football academy and works as a talent scout) and the supernatural, and his expert eye had noticed something amiss. After an impressive dash, he caught the Senegal goalkeeper Tony Sylva by surprise and took possession of an apparently innocuous, previously unnoticed object that was lying in the net. Quick to cotton on to what was happening, the crowd began to roar. It was as if Nigeria had drawn level. They did just that six minutes from the end with a goal by Julius Agahowa, who grabbed a second in extra time, thus taking Nigeria into the semi-finals. Laloko was subsequently suspended for a year but his sacrifice had been worthwhile.

Two years later in Mali, in another African Cup of Nations, the same Senegalese keeper, Tony Sylva, stayed unbeaten for 448 minutes. It was a notable achievement but, naturally enough, popular legend attributed it not to the sound defensive tactics of Metsu or to the ability of the Monaco number one, but to the *feticheur* who greased Sylva's goalposts with ointment before the match with Zambia. At the interval, of course, Sylva changed ends and in subsequent matches changed stadiums and even cities, but that is beside the point. The beneficial effects of the potion evidently followed the Senegalese number one everywhere he went – though it failed to prevent his team losing the final against Cameroon.

In Mali there's a *fetiche* market not far from the Modibo Keita Stadium. It is apparently the haunt of footballers who go there to buy the tools of their trade at competitive prices. Three and a half euros for an elephant's tooth to put in your sock if you are a goalkeeper ('How can you hope to score against an elephant?' says the vendor). Four euros for a monkey's head, ten or so for a caiman's head, seven for a handful of porcupine spines (purposes unspecified). Down at the *fetiche* market, they reckon France's wins in the 1998 World Cup (against an off-form Brazil) and in the European Championship in 2000 (against Italy in a dramatic final) were down to the wiles of Aguib Sosso, the Mali *muti*-man. Sosso died in 2000 and since then *Les Bleus* have struggled a lot and won nothing. Without him, in the 2002 World Cup against connoisseurs of magic like the Senegalese, France could only lose. Which is what they did.

Witch doctors can work in your favour, but also against you. Any commitments to them have to be honoured. When Ivory Coast won their only African Cup of Nations in Senegal in 1992 after an interminable penalty shoot-out in the final against Ghana, a group of witch doctors turned up at the offices of FIF, the Ivorian federation, demanding money. Inebriated by success, the officials told them what to do with their claims and chased them away. The magicians were annoyed and pronounced a highly potent anathema on the Elephants, who subsequently went through an awful patch.

In 2000, after being knocked out of the Cup of Nations in the first round, the players were locked up in a military camp for days, subjected to forced marches and obliged to read literature about patriotism and the valour of the shirt, the flag, the regime and the people. The bad spell lasted until 2005, when the team qualified for the World Cup for the first time, ahead of Cameroon, who missed a decisive penalty with the last kick of their last game against Egypt. What was the reason for such a fortunate yet brilliant resurrection? Simple – the Ivorian government had at last resolved the diplomatic/magical incident of more than ten years earlier by sending defence minister Moise Lida Kouassi to the village just outside Abidjan whence the Elephants' benefactors had come in 1992. The witch doctors accepted the minister's peace offering of a bottle of whisky and $2,000. Try telling the Ivorians that people who follow the national team with such passion had nothing to do with Cameroonian Pierre Wome's penalty hitting the post. The Wome episode needs to be reconsidered in the light of the following words. 'I say that magic doesn't exist in football. Proof of the fact is that Cameroon isn't the most advanced country in terms of magic but it's better at football than the likes of Benin, Togo and Nigeria, nations in which magic is well rooted.' So said Roger Milla to *France Football* in 1981.

Ghana qualified for the final stages of the World Cup for the first time in 2005. The country has always been good at football, winning the African Cup of Nations four times, but had never managed to reach the World Cup finals. According to Joshua Nyame, a pastor in the western region of the country, this was due to the fact that a negative influence was weighing on the Black Stars. He claimed, naturally enough, that he had the technical and spiritual means to chase away this presence and was prepared to perform the *sunsumuade*, the required ritual, in return for the right fee. Through two presenters at Happy FM, a local radio station, Nyame got in touch with Stephen Appiah, the former Juventus player and captain of the national team, who decided to pay to 'liberate' the Black Stars.

The payment was to be made in two instalments: the first of five million cedis, the second of ten million, making a total of the equivalent of just over €1,300. Ghana had to win away against South Africa and promptly succeeded in doing so. 'It was a foregone conclusion,' declared Nyame to the Kokrokoo Morning programme on Peace FM, another popular radio station in Accra and environs. 'I sent my 22 angels to South Africa and ordered them to play alongside the Black Stars. That's why the *Bafana Bafana* lost 2-0.' In view of the victory, pastor Nyame demanded another 100 million cedis and started to bombard Appiah with phone calls. The captain got fed up and cut off all contacts with the preacher. The scene seemed set for a retaliatory gesture. But no, Ghana qualified for Germany 2006 and when Nyame stormed into the studios of Peace FM to receive his just reward on live radio, listeners sent in text messages to insult him.

Ghana isn't new to controversy in the sphere of the supernatural. Samuel Kuffour had one of his many quarrels with the Ghanaian federation over pre-match propitiatory rites. A few years back, the former Bayern Munich and Roma defender got very het up indeed when he discovered some of his national team mates carrying out certain practices – stuffing their socks with amulets, spreading powder in the dressing rooms, swallowing strange potions – that had little to do with the classic pre-match warm-up. Kuffour, who had lived for almost ten years in Germany, has always run off a short fuse and he expressed his perplexity the only way he knows how. The defender pointed out the gap that separated people like him, who had spent many years in Europe, from some of his younger team-mates, who were still playing in Ghana. He told the youngsters they were gullible provincials. But he did so in such an unpleasant tone that he was kicked out of the national team for a while. He had to apologise before he was allowed to return. The local journalists said he had offended the nation.

In general, players who come to Europe have difficulty in accepting and understanding certain things. To some of their compatriots they can seem presumptuous and arrogant, lackeys in the service of the white man. Today, though, there are many youngsters in African national sides who were brought up in Europe and have never even been to Africa. In such cases, the gap between those who believe in and are keen to practise certain rites to win the favour of the gods and others who only want to play football grows wider – unless you've been successful in Europe thanks to the beneficial influx of a drop of holy water or two.

Magic in small doses
'Going off for a major competition without consulting or taking a witch doctor is like sitting an exam without a pen.'
African Soccer magazine

South African footballer: 'There was a period in which every-thing was going badly. So one of the officials made us get into a minibus and took us out of town into the woods. When we got off we found ourselves in front of a termites' nest. The *muti*-man uncovered it, removed all the soil from the inside and poured in a magic potion. We then had to take off our clothes and get into it naked. Then we had walk back to the minibus without turning round. The results followed.'

Frederick Musisi, a former Uganda international, now a journalist: 'Often, when the ball hits the post or the bar, players from the attacking team go and touch the exact spot hit by the ball. They think that by doing this they'll remove the spell that someone has cast. It's not unusual to urinate on the pitch. Players who do this think it's a way to wash away a curse.'

Papa Bouba Diop, the Senegal and Portsmouth midfield player, formerly of Fulham: 'Magic is practised in the part of the world I come from. I'm used to certain rituals and after my intervention we immediately got results. If necessary, we'll do it again.' What had Papa Diop been up to at Craven Cottage in December 2004? He had performed a voodoo rite in which he had scattered a mixture of animal blood, incense and soil. Six victories and three draws in the last ten home games of the season, two penalties saved by Edwin van der Sar against Aston Villa (final score 1-1) and a great start to the year 2005 with three home wins, the second in the last minute with a goal from Bouba Diop himself after withstanding a long siege by West Bromwich Albion.

Recently the Tanzanian football association handed out fines of $500 each to the country's two leading teams, Simba and Yanga, after their players had been involved in a series of surreal episodes before and after a match in Dar es Salaam. Two Yanga players obeyed their magician's exhortation to urinate on a precise spot on the pitch where it appeared Simba had placed an amulet. The Yanga captain, John Paul Masanja, had refused to shake the hand of the opposing captain, Seleman Matola. Nothing personal, Masanja said, he was acting under instructions though he did not explain why. The two teams had caused the kick-off to be delayed by half an hour because they disagreed on who should take the field first.

Again in Tanzania, two years before a vital match against Kenya. The national team members saw a witch doctor get on to their bus in place of the director who was supposed to pay them their agreed match bonus. All the money had gone to the *muti*-man. Kenya won 3-0 and the witch doctor ended up getting the blame.

In Zambia, Profund Warriors FC seemed unbeatable at home. They were on a long winning streak. Their opponents reacted accordingly. They started to change on their buses, no longer in the away team dressing rooms. They also avoided entering the stadium through the entrance reserved to them and climbed over the surrounding fence. It was a bold move but it worked. Profund Warriors starting losing to everybody.

Terry Paine, formerly of Southampton and England, who went to coach in South Africa: 'I was about to walk into the dressing room when my players asked me not to. "There's a *muti* over the door," they said. Who cares, I thought, and despite their begging me not to, I opened the door and walked in. We lost 1-0, after 17 matches without a defeat.'

14. From Khartoum to Zurich

Khartoum, February 8, 1957. The delegates of the football associations of Egypt, Ethiopia, South Africa and Sudan meet in the Sudanese capital. Thirteen people sit at the table and – to return to the subject of superstition – the number brings bad luck. The four countries bring into being the Confederation of African Football and launch the first African Cup of Nations which is to be played over the days ahead. All seems to be proceeding well and enthusiasm abounds. African football is at last on the move.

The first problem crops up in the afternoon and it is eventually solved in 1992. In the first African Cup of Nations, South Africa want to field an all-white team. The other delegates, 12 out of 13, stonewall and South Africa are expelled from the confederation. Ethiopia, who should have played them in the semi-final, go directly into the final, which they lose against Egypt. South Africa are victims of their own segregationist policy. A year earlier, the South African Minister of the Interior, Eben Dönges, had drawn up a draft programme for apartheid as applied to sport. The basic idea was to raise insurmountable barriers, directing whites towards rugby and cricket, blacks towards football and boxing.

The newborn CAF's reaction was rapid, incisive and adamant but the rest of the sporting world was less determined in its condemnation of South Africa's horrendous policy. In 1960 CAF expelled South Africa, whereas in 1961 FIFA merely suspended the country and lifted the ban two years later under its British president Sir Stanley Rous. South Africa had made the FIFA officials a promise: for the 1966 World Cup they would field an all-white team but then they would begin a racial turnover and pick an all-black team in 1970. It may sound like a macabre comedy, but Rous and his cronies initially liked the idea. Fortunately, the love affair did not last long. In 1964 FIFA suspended South Africa again, but only expelled the country in 1976, 16 years after CAF and six years after the International Olympic Committee (South African athletes had competed in the Olympic Games for the last time in Rome in 1960).

On July 10, 1991, the IOC announced that the South Africans would be readmitted to the Olympics at Barcelona the following year. On July 3, 1992, South Africa were allowed back into FIFA and four days later in Durban the newborn *Bafana Bafana* – a Zulu expression meaning 'boys' – took the field against Cameroon, winning 1-0 with a penalty by Doctor Khumalo. Exile had formally come to an end, as had apartheid, which FW de Klerk's National Party government had set about dismantling in 1990. But all the country's problems remained.

Nelson Mandela was freed on February 11, 1990, after almost 26 years in jail. On May 10, 1994, a few hours after commencing his mandate as president, Madiba – as he is known to all South Africans, after the name of his clan in the Xhosa tribe – turned up at Johannesburg's Ellis Park, a landmark of ultra-white rugby, to watch the South Africa v Zambia football match. Mandela's positive influence was being felt in every sector, sport included.

The new South African president legitimised first rugby, then cricket. In 1995 the Rainbow Nation organised the rugby World Cup and hosted a cricket Test series against England. South Africa won both and Mandela handed out the prizes, wearing first Boer Springbok captain François Pienaar's shirt, then the blazer and cap of Hansie Cronje, another white captain and a symbol of South African cricket. Mandela's policy was almost one of annexation. To forget apartheid and attempt to heal the wounds inflicted over half a century, there could no longer be a distinction between white sports and black sports. Mandela completed his hat-trick on February 3, 1996, at the FNB Stadium in Soweto, better known as Soccer City, the ground that six years earlier had met the Mandela rally with an ecstatic welcome and in which the newly released leader had made his first speech to the nation – a politically and emotionally powerful declaration of intent.

On that day in 1996 *Bafana Bafana* won the African Cup of Nations. Everyone gave the credit to 'Madiba's Magic', Madiba having turned up in the grandstand wearing the shirt of Neil Tovey, the white *Bafana Bafana* captain. It was an unforgettable scene and I was lucky enough to be there to report the event for three different Italian dailies (it's a hard life being a freelance journalist), *Il Manifesto, Il Giornale* and *La Repubblica*: one leftwing, one rightwing and one centre.

For Mandela the No 9 shirt of captain Neil Tovey, for his grand-daughter Rochelle the No 15 of Doctor Khumalo. When the Imilanji Kantu chorus began to sing the national anthem *Nkosi Sikelel'Africa* (God Bless Africa), 80,000 voices and 80,000 closed fists rose to the sky. The gates of Soccer City opened at six in the morning and the stand opposite where I was sitting was full by ten. There were umbrellas used as parasols, iced beer, rivers of whisky. Outside the stadium ten rand (£2.50) half-litre bottles of Martell were selling like hot cakes. At 1.30pm the third place play-off between Zambia and Ghana kicked off. After Zambia's 1-0 victory, the closing ceremony commenced. Bob Mabena played his ambient dub at every stoppage... as on the opening day, music played a fundamental role. Despite the heat and an hour-long wait, dancing carried on without respite.
Il Manifesto, February 4, 1994

After success in 'white sports', triumph in the African Cup of Nations came as a breath of fresh air for blacks because football is their sport. It ended as it had begun with Nelson Mandela as the star of the show. On the opening day, the president had sent a message to *Bafana Bafana*, asking them for commitment in this first footballing encounter between Africa and South Africa. The 'Boys' kept their word and yesterday the president was on the field again, after going to see the team in their hotel before the semi-final and on the eve of the final. He was his usual charismatic self. When he entered the stadium, the 80,000 spectators exploded. Madiba sat in the Super Suite, alongside vice-president De Klerk, the Zulu king Goodwill Zwelethini and the leader of the opposition party Mangosuthu Buthelezi.

In the dressing rooms, the manager Clive Barker, a white man, put the triumph in its proper context: 'It's an outstanding day for our country. This victory is more important than the ones we have achieved in rugby and cricket, because football is our true national sport.' This is a half-truth since football is, above all, the sport of blacks, but it has the merit of clarifying the true significance of the victory. At last, whites had been seen inside a football stadium again. True, they were a minority, but they were there. And Mandela's call for *Bafana Bafana* to identify with the 'one team, one nation' concept appears to have been picked up by the nation. Yet again the South African president's charisma has caught the feelings of his citizens.

La Repubblica, February 4, 1994

The 1996 Cup was magical. I had come to South Africa full of hopes and expectations, which were fulfilled. I found a country of contradictions, scarred by apartheid, a country in many ways in intensive care. To achieve integration the government had established precise employment quotas: so many whites, so many blacks, so many mixed race and so on. The idea, which was a good one to begin with, proved hard to implement. Paradoxically, people were being employed to do jobs they knew nothing about and, as they picked up the ropes, quasi-comic situations were occurring. To cite an example from the world of football, take the African Cup of Nations television commentaries. For the first time in the history of the country, the commentary was not only in English (by two blacks, incidentally) but also in Afrikaans, *de facto* a white language.

Yet since it was necessary to please everyone, commentaries were also broadcast in Zulu, Xhosa, Sotho and Tswana, the country's other most widely spoken languages. That makes six in all. Not that there were six channels, one for each. No, seeing that a match lasts 90 minutes, it was decided to allot them a quarter of an hour each. The result? A pointless and incomprehensible babel, a chaotic oral representation of the Rainbow Nation – all its colours, all its races, all its languages. And are there people capable of understanding all six of the tongues? At a conservative estimate, maybe a dozen in all South Africa. In short, everyone was confused in the name of integration.

One day on the beach in Durban I met an Italian TV commentator and a producer who were following the Cup, chatting to a white girl.

I joined in. After ten minutes we were arguing. The girl, who was no older than 25, was nonchalantly nostalgic about the days when the beach had been out of bounds to blacks. I did believe what I was hearing. She really believed in what she was saying. I had been travelling round South Africa for a month but I had not met a single mixed-race couple. I would hear whites whistle to attract the attention of black waiters, I would see the walls of whites' houses protected, trench-like, with razor wire.

I would meet blacks who were venomous with whites, incapable of accepting people who, until recently, had treated them as if they had the plague, as fellow citizens. I read about blacks killing each other *en masse* to share out the power finally at their disposal after years of apartheid. The country was badly in need of massive doses of Madiba's Magic. Wearing rugby or football shirts to promote the embrace between black and white could help, but it was insufficient. The whites had behaved too badly for everything to fall into place in a hurry.

Forced integration. When I first went to South Africa in the summer of 1995 to buy photos for the Panini album, the country was plastered with posters for the rugby World Cup. The main image used was of Chester Williams, the only black player in the Springboks team. It was something of a strained interpretation – it was as if Williams was the only player in the whole competition – but it was, in a sense, understandable. The truth came out a few years later.

> In 1995 Chester Williams was the symbol of multiracial South Africa, the only black player in the rugby team who won the World Cup at home; Nelson Mandela, released from prison only in 1990, raised the trophy in the jersey of François Pienaar, a 100 per cent Afrikaaner. Seven years on, Chester Williams has decided to spill the beans about those years and that national side, wiping the slate clean of multiracial rhetoric. *Chester, Biography of Courage* was published in South Africa on October 28, 2002, and it has certainly created a stir. Williams recounts that, as a black rugby player, he was not only grudgingly put up with by his white team-mates but also that he was used by officials to restore to rugby, a white sport par excellence, the purity it had lost in decades of barred entry to black athletes.

Williams tells how on away trips and during training camps with the team, he always used to eat alone, while the others ate together. His team-mate James Small called him a 'fucking kaffir', one of the commonest white insults for blacks in South Africa. 'Why do you want to play our game. You know you can't play it.' Through his lawyer, Small has announced that he has no precise recollection of the episodes described by Williams. 'They only tolerated us in the team because it made them look as though they had embraced change,' says Williams. 'You know, much of it was born of the belief that being white in South Africa somehow made you superior to anyone born black. It could never occur to them that a black player could be better than a white.' According to Williams, by pretending to accept blacks South African rugby in the Nineties won international consensus without repudiating its strongest racist convictions. Since 1999 South African rugby teams have been obliged to name four black players in a squad of 22. It is significant that, to date, no club has ever exceeded its quota, and that in the past ten years only 13 blacks have been selected for the Springboks.

In 1999, after two bad injuries, Chester Williams was back on top form but was not picked for the national team. Nick Mallett, the coach at the time, told him he had enough black players, that the government quota had been reached, that it was pointless calling up any more blacks. 'In all my playing years, most white players and coaches believed that a black selection weakened the team.' If Mandela had shoulders broad enough to bear the weight of an entire nation, in 1995 Chester Williams was a mere youngster whose speed had allowed him to shine on the wing for the Springboks. In the lead-up to the World Cup, the face of Williams, the 'Black Pearl', was to be seen all over South Africa. 'The wait is over' ran the advertising slogan. The Cape Coloured (as he would have been called under apartheid) from Paarl made the best of a bad job. 'Often I just used to smile about it.' A the training camp the barbs kept coming in. 'Nothing malicious', says Williams, who just grinned and bore it.

Immediately prior to the World Cup, Williams got injured
and missed the first matches. In the quarter-finals he was
called up to replace Pieter Hendricks, suspended for punching
a Canadian opponent. The Canada match had cast a bad light
on the Springboks, and the news of the selection distracted the
world press from the stink caused by his team-mates. In the
quarter-final against Western Samoa, Williams scored four
tries. In the post-match press conference the Samoans accused
the South Africans of making racist remarks in the scrum.
'How can they make such a slur?' demanded the Springboks'
skipper Pienaar. 'Can't they see that one of our team-mates
is black?' Williams, sitting beside Pienaar, smiled. Williams
was forced out of the game by injury at the age of 32. So why
did he not speak out before? 'I was just not the kind of guy who
rocked the boat. And I just saw too many black players who
spoke out then seeing their career finished. If you wanted to
get on, you put up and shut up.'
Corriere della Sera, November 22, 2002

Certain obscenities still seem hard to eradicate at a social level. In
March 2001 SAFA, the South African Football Federation, decided to
switch a 2002 World Cup qualifying match between *Bafana Bafana*
and Zimbabwe from Cape Town to Johannesburg to protest against the
Cape Town city council's decision, a few months earlier, to ban football
teams from using the best sports facility in the city. The inhabitants
of Newlands, a white residential neighbourhood, did not welcome the
crowds of blacks who came regularly to watch the matches there. But
there was no problem about playing cricket and rugby matches in the
same stadium. SAFA's reaction was strong and determined. 'We are not
going to ask for permits to play football,' said Danny Jordaan, a former
African National Congress MP, head of the federation and the man
responsible for the campaign to stage the World Cup. 'These pieces of
paper remind us of the past when, to travel round the city, we used to
have to carry special permits and identity documents in our pockets
issued by a regime that governed by apartheid.'

The 1996 African Cup of Nations was awarded to South Africa for
political reasons. The 20th edition of the tournament had been given to

Kenya but CAF took it away from them in 1995. The country was behind schedule with the building of the stadiums and infrastructure needed to host a tournament that was to be extended from 12 to 16 teams. Kenya were having problems and CAF was very keen to hand the cup to South Africa. It was urgently necessary to show the world that Africa was capable of organising a World Cup and, as far as the organisation of major events is concerned, for the rest of the world Africa could only mean South Africa – a country of big hotels, golf courses, wine, safaris and clean, well appointed beaches. Seen from the north, it seemed to be the least African country in Africa, hence the most reassuring, the best organised, the best prepared, the closest to western standards. What a mistake that was. And it was largely down to the Africans themselves. They proclaimed South Africa as their guiding nation. But it was a country that, until a few years previously, had turned its back on the rest of the continent. The 1996 African Cup of Nations laid bare all the problems of a place that was trying to come to terms with an enormous tragedy. Forget all about telecommunications, western-style organisation, large hotels and modern transport: the tournament was to be organised much better in Burkina Faso two years later.

Be that as it may, the Cup was assigned to South Africa. But in November 1995, just when it was about to begin, things took a bad turn with Nelson Mandela's condemnation of the Nigerian regime for the hanging of the dissident writer Ken Saro-Wiwa, a candidate for the Nobel Prize for Literature, and eight colleagues. Mandela had Nigeria suspended from the Commonwealth. In retaliation the military regime in Lagos and Abuja, among other things, refused to send their team, the winners of the African Cup of Nations two years before, to South Africa. This international political incident had a significant effect on the tournament.

Despite all these difficulties, the Cup in South Africa set an unstoppable mechanism into motion: the process that was supposed to take the World Cup to Africa, or rather, as CAF and FIFA officials believed, to South Africa. A few months earlier, the continent had won the right to send five teams, no longer just three, to the World Cup finals. It is a ridiculous percentage if you think that South America has only ten federations but is entitled to four and a half places, whereas Africa boasts 53 federations. But when it comes to electing the president of FIFA, however mistreated and neglected they are, those 53 federations are worth 53 votes. It is a fact Sepp Blatter knew only too well.

Two years later, in June 1998, FIFA had to elect its new president. After 14 years of unopposed power, the Brazilian João Havelange had given up the post. At first the only candidate to succeed him was Lennart Johansson of Sweden, the president of UEFA. In March Blatter appeared from behind the scenes to announce his own candidature. He had been planning this *coup de théâtre* for months, busily lobbying to win the largely economic support of federations such as Qatar and Saudi Arabia, then, thanks to Havelange, of the South American countries and ultimately to make inroads into Africa's united front. CAF president Issa Hayatou had promised Johansson his continent's 53 votes but due to a combination of tireless travel, promises and dodgy dealings – subsequently denounced by journalists and writers such as Andrew Jennings and David Yallop – Blatter was able to poach some of them for himself. He eventually beat Johansson by 111 votes to 80. Among his promises were the staging of the 1999 Under-20 World Cup in Nigeria, a place where no one wanted to go, and the assignment of the 2006 World Cup finals to South Africa.

The voting for the 2006 World Cup finals was held over two days in Zurich in June 2000. I reported the event for the Italian daily *Il Manifesto*.

> Today in Zurich FIFA will pick the country to organise the 2006 World Cup finals. Originally five countries were competing but on Monday the number dropped to four when Brazil withdrew and announced they would vote for South Africa. The other three competing countries are Germany, England and Morocco.
>
> For the first time in the history of football, Africa has tangible chances of success. Applying the precepts of divide and rule, and through a clever policy of miscellaneous promises, Sepp Blatter managed to break the collective solidarity of the African nations, ensuring himself the votes needed to achieve the presidency of FIFA. Now the moment has come for him to pay off his debts. Since he was elected, the FIFA president has done nothing else but repeat that the time is ripe for Africa, that it is necessary to adopt a continent-by-continent rotation,

that after America (USA 1994), Europe (France 1998) and Asia (Japan-Korea 2002), Africa's turn will come in 2006.

British bookmakers make South Africa favourites, ahead of England, Germany and Morocco, but the outcome of the ballot is anything but a foregone conclusion. In the meantime, the big surprise is that Africa now has two bidders, with South Africa, who have long been in the running, now being joined by Morocco, making their third attempt to host the World Cup following vain efforts for 1994 and 1998. This has obviously shifted the balance since the Arab countries are now behind their Moroccan brothers. The double candidature has caught CAF off guard. Officially, the African confederation is in favour of a World Cup in Africa, without expressing preferences as to where, but behind the scenes an all-out war has been waged.

Twenty-four votes will be cast by eight European delegates, four Asians, three South Americans, three North and Central Americans, one Oceanian and Blatter. The voting will be held over three ballots with the first two countries in the second going on to the last. The delegates come from important countries but also from minor ones such as Malta. This is why teams are suddenly playing in friendlies against the tiny Mediterranean island's national team. Both South Africa and England have been to Malta to celebrate the centenary of its football federation – a classic example of an invitation you cannot refuse. For the record, *Bafana Bafana* turned up on Malta with 13 players, including two goalkeepers, and made a poor showing. Also worth mentioning are the courtesy visits made first by Bobby Charlton, then by Franz Beckenbauer, to Mali, another country with the right to vote.

Looking at the four candidates, it has to be said that Germany, powerful from a number of points of view, is paying for the fact that it hosted the World Cup in 1974. It looks like England, who hosted the Cup in 1966 and showed their mettle again in 1996 when they organised the European Championship, will pay a very high price for the hooligan phenomenon. Events at the 2000 European Championship have probably scuppered their candidature for good. Then there are the African countries, among whom South Africa is the favourite over Morocco. The only weak point for the land of Mandela is security. South Africa is not one of the calmest countries on the planet and the football world knows that. Now Germany, who in the last few hours seem to have won the role as South Africa's main rival, are focusing totally on the security factor. Otherwise, South Africa have everything going for them: infrastructure (hotels and stadiums), testimonials of the calibre of Nelson Mandela, money, important friendships (not only Blatter but also Pelé) and experience, having already organised the rugby and cricket World Cups. Morocco, for their part, can count on virtually total security. The Maghreb country seems way behind in terms of organisation, however. Thanks to tourism, they have big hotels – albeit not nationwide – but they lack stadiums, infrastructure and the know-how needed to host a giant event like a World Cup with 32 participants.

One obstacle to the choice of an African country could be FIFA's fear of making a second consecutive leap in the dark after Korea-Japan 2002. The dual Asian solution was rejected by Blatter two years before it actually happened. At FIFA they realised they had committed a big mistake in terms both of the choice of the single candidates and of the combination of the two, a test that failed even before it started.

This consideration leads to another. It cannot be ruled out that by pulling out the umpteenth rabbit from his bottomless hat, Blatter will assign Europe the 2006 World Cup and the 2010 edition to South Africa, thereby seeking to satisfy all concerned (aside from Brazil). Just last Monday, this way out was encouraged by Franz Beckenbauer: Teutonic tradition to shore up the shaking foundations of FIFA in the short term, and ten years for Africa to organise her World Cup.
Il Manifesto, July 6, 2000

That day in Zurich conjurer Sepp Blatter's rabbit really did come out of the hat. Or at least its ears did. The rest of it appeared four years later.

The German police have won because they are more efficient than South Africa's. Or at least that is what they think at FIFA. Yesterday the job of organising the 2006 World Cup was assigned. On the shortlist were Germany, England, South Africa and Morocco. Tradition versus emotion. If Morocco, at their third consecutive attempt after defeats against the USA (1994) and France (1998), appeared to have slender chances of success, South Africa looked like the favourite in this strange race. That is how the infallible British bookmakers saw it too. But the ball is round even at the FIFA headquarters and it was Germany who came out on top. South Africa's Achilles heel was its poor security and it was there that, with customary mastery, Franz Beckenbauer, head of the German delegation, stuck his arrow. It was a lethal shot. Europe has gained its tenth World Cup finals, maintaining an average of one in every two. In the meantime, Africa will have to wait. So much for the continent-by-continent rotation invoked by Sepp Blatter.

After victory on the field in 1974 and on the bench in 1990, yesterday marked yet another success for Kaiser Franz. Thanks above all to a truly perfect presentation, Beckenbauer came from the rear to win in the final sprint. Germany turned up in Zurich with Chancellor Gerhard Schroeder, Claudia Schiffer, Boris Becker and Jürgen Klinsmann. All of them behind the Kaiser. South Africa brought a video of Nelson Mandela. Beckenbauer worked like only great lobbyists know how. He said it was a scandal when Brazil withdrew from the race last Monday and announced they would support South Africa. He even threatened to withdraw himself. His tears were a ploy to distract attention from the outflanking manoeuvres that, in the meantime, were growing more and more intense.

The Germans set out to curb the Africanist sentimentalism that seemed to have captured the hearts of so many FIFA delegates. It was thus that the security saga started. South Africa – devastated by a civil war, bloodthirsty gangs in action day and night in every corner of the country, the safety of the delegates, players and fans at serious risk. The cry of alarm grew louder and, in the long run, it worked.

The defeat has not gone down well, not only in South Africa but throughout the black continent. Danny Jordaan, head of the South African delegation, has spoken of FIFA's sheep and goats, the first well nourished, the second left to die without food. According to Jordaan, organising the World Cup would have earned South Africa $2.5 billion and created 130,000 jobs. Roger Milla, the unforgettable leader of the Indomitable Lions of Cameroon and member of the South African committee, has asked African national sides to boycott the 2006 World Cup. The president of South Africa, Thabo Mbeki, spoke of a 'tragic day'. Nelson Mandela released no comments but his face, which appeared on television shortly after the Zurich announcement, said much more than any banal phrase.

In Zurich itself, one contender was knocked out after each of the three rounds. Morocco was the first to go. Germany started very strongly, winning ten votes. South Africa followed with six, England with five. After receiving just three preferences, Morocco sadly dropped out. England were eliminated ingloriously in the second ballot, their two votes a pittance compared with Germany and South Africa's 11 apiece. The sons of the Queen caused their own downfall. In a match that was being fought out on the playing field of security, the weak point of the South Africans and hobbyhorse of the Germans, the English were not even allowed into the dressing-rooms. The hooligans showed all their power a fortnight ago in the European Championship in Belgium and Holland, suggesting that, if there was any need to be reminded, the phenomenon is anything but under control. That was enough to shatter England's World Cup dreams.

On to the third and decisive ballot, Germany and South Africa fought over the two votes that went to England in the second. One candidate voted for Germany, the other suddenly abstained. So victory went to Germany. If the second vote had gone to South Africa, at 12 each the secretary general of FIFA, Sepp Blatter, would have been obliged to cast the deciding vote. That would have forced him to come out into the open, a situation he wanted to avoid at all costs.

The FIFA delegate who decided the fate of the 2006 World Cup has been identified. It turned out to be Charles Dempsey, the elderly president of the Oceania confederation. Only he and David Will of Scotland had voted for England in the second ballot. If we take for granted that Will subsequently backed the other European candidate, Germany, then it stands to reason that it was Dempsey who made the decisive abstention. It is laughable that a delegate from New Zealand should be able to decide where the World Cup finals are played. It is football we are talking about here, not yachting or rugby.

All that South Africa can do now is try again in 2010. Beckenbauer had already predicted as much on Monday: Germany in 2006, South Africa in 2010. The first part of his prophecy has come true. It remains to be seen for the second. In four years many things can happen.

Il Manifesto, July 11, 2000

Blatter conducted proceedings like a true maestro. How could the World Cup be taken away from South Africa without losing the friendship and, above all, the votes of Africa (new FIFA presidential elections were looming in 2002)? Hence the brainwave of *deus ex machina* Charles Dempsey. The old timer probably knows damn all about football but he certainly saved puppet master Blatter from a sticky situation. Waiting for the New Zealander, who fled with all Africa chasing after him, were a golden pension and life membership of FIFA, granted to him at the end of the Seoul Congress in 2002. Germany received the 2006 World Cup and South Africa received another promise. This time it was kept. In 2002 Blatter was re-elected, shaking off the competition of the African candidate, Issa Hayatou, by 139 votes to 56, and announced that 2010 will be the year of the World Cup in Africa. Continent-by-continent rotation had officially commenced.

Five countries applied: South Africa, Morocco, Egypt, Tunisia and Libya. The last two tried jointly at first, then, when FIFA dismissed the idea of a repeat of a two-nation organisation, they competed separately. So the vote-gathering bandwagon set off again. Libya invited journalists to Monte Carlo to meet the federation president Al Saadi, Colonel Gaddafi's son, who was then a player with Udinese after two years at Perugia (he only played ten minutes in Serie A, against Juventus, a club in which he held a seven per cent stake). Morocco, making their fourth attempt in a row (in 1987 they lost to the United States by a single vote) invited journalists to visit their country. South Africa did not this time because they had done so four years earlier and we all know how things turned out then. I went to Morocco for *Il Corriere della Sera*. I learnt that only 12 kilometres separate the country from Spain. If they could, the members of the Morocco 2010 committee would have built a bridge between the two countries just to prove that Morocco is actually part of Europe.

'The new Morocco is ready for the World Cup.' The slogan is like a mantra that the cosmopolitan delegation assembled to take the 2010 World Cup to the southern shore of the Mediterranean keeps repeating to itself. On May 15, in Zurich, a piece of football history will be made. The 24 FIFA delegates with the right to vote (no Italians among them) will choose the African country that will host the 2010 World Cup, the first ever for the continent. Speaking realistically, it is going to be a duel between South Africa and Morocco. Morocco have come from behind but are gaining ground day by day. 'We like being the underdogs, it will make victory all the sweeter.' So said Bob Stiles, head of security for Morocco 2010, the same role he played at USA 1994.

He was in Morocco with Alan Rothenberg, the man who organised the American World Cup finals and guided the FIFA visits to the countries shortlisted for the organisation of the 2006 World Cup. Morocco was one of those countries, but it was 'old' Morocco. Today so many things have changed. For example, the new king, Mohamed VI, on the throne since 1999, has guaranteed rights for women unthinkable in any other Islamic country. In the Moroccan parliament sit three women ministers, and the country's member of the International Olympic Committee is also a woman. In Morocco you see women wearing the burka, but also girls riding about on scooters as you would in any European city. Interpreting the guidelines of the Koran is also left to the responsibility of individuals. Hence many Moroccans drink alcohol.

Security is one of the strong points of Morocco's candidature, especially in view of the situation in South Africa, where cities such as Johannesburg and Durban are extremely dangerous and murders, thefts and shootings are common. In Morocco, only 15 citizens in 1000 commit crimes – few countries in the world can boast such a low percentage – firearms are conspicuous by their absence, 90 per cent of crimes are committed by youths and over 90 per cent of cases are solved.

If in South Africa Aids is rife, in Morocco only 0.8 per cent of the population is infected, an unattainable figure for South Africa. Then there is the short 12 kilometre gap between Spain and Morocco, meaning proximity, unity and hospitality, other key words for Morocco 2010. Casablanca is three hours by air from the major European capitals. Six of the eight cities selected to host the World Cup are located together in a small area. The longest distance, 900 kilometres from Tangiers to Agadir, takes 45 minutes by air. The roads are in excellent condition and rail transport, already fair, will be raised to European standards. On the telecommunications front, Morocco has always led the way in Africa: in 1994 it was one of the first ten countries in the world to introduce GSM, the global system for mobile phone communication. Tourism is one of the country's major resources: the four splendid imperial cities, the capital Rabat, Fes, Meknes and Marrakesh, plus Casablanca and Tangiers, are used to welcoming large numbers of people.

Of the nine stadiums earmarked to host the competition, three are ready, three are being built and three are waiting for the outcome of the vote on May 15. Funding is not a problem. The government has ensured its support by depositing €140 million in a Swiss bank account. The estimated budget allocated for the World Cup is €378m, €271m of which should return through ticket sales. The remaining €107m is also guaranteed by the government. All this will enable Morocco to achieve something significant for Africa. A fund called Football Sans Frontières will be set up into which the money received from FIFA will be deposited. The fund will serve to

develop African football – and not only football. 'This will be the first World Cup to be staged in Africa and we believe it is only right that the whole continent should reap the benefits.'
Corriere della Sera, February 22, 2004

Although I had not been invited to South Africa, I was keen to treat everybody equally, so I called Danny Jordaan, the man who had been working untiringly for years to take the World Cup to his country.

Danny Jordaan knows how things are done. This year the head of the South Africa 2010 committee is celebrating ten years of World Cup lobbying. Since 1994, the year in which he was elected to the South African parliament as a member of the African National Congress, his main job has been to take the World Cup to the Rainbow Nation. Three years in parliament have been followed by seven travelling round the world. That on top of a career as a first-rate footballer and cricketer, and 15 years spent running the history department at Dower College in the Eastern Cape.

'Ten years chasing the World Cup, I reckon it's a record, and a hard one to beat at that.'

Today South Africa are favourites in the race to organise the 2010 World Cup, Africa's first.

'I don't feel like the favourite. Whatever FIFA says is fine by me but I personally only think about working to persuade delegates that South Africa is the right choice. I'll only feel easy after the vote.'

Do you think a sense of guilt for what happened four years ago can play in South Africa's favour?

'No, you don't assign a World Cup out of compassion or to right a past wrong. We've started from scratch against new rivals, and we're ready to work even harder to bring home a result.'

Morocco, your main rival, has put a top-class delegation in place. The impression one gets from the outside is that you have to do everything by yourself.

'It's a mistaken impression. I'm backed by the government,

by former footballers [Abedi Pelé, Roger Milla] and of course by Nelson Mandela, our inspiration.'

What are the points in South Africa's favour?

'Infrastructure: stadiums, transport, accommodation. Then telecommunications with the television and newspaper boom and, last but not least, the fact that our country has the strongest economy in the whole of the African continent. Then there's tourism, which is one of our greatest resources. That means excellent roads, railways and easy access to airports in all the 11 cities we've chosen for the World Cup.'

Compared to her competitors, South Africa can count on much greater experience.

'In the last ten years, we have organised 11 major sporting events: the rugby World Cup, the African Cup of Nations, the cricket World Cup, to cite just a few examples. We can regard ourselves as experts on the subject of event organisation and it shouldn't be forgotten that we were all ready to host the 2006 World Cup. FIFA had given its OK and we only lost by a whisker, battling it out to the last with Germany, a country that's second to none when it comes to organisation.'

Weak points? Your competitors point their fingers at security and health.

'I've been hearing these questions about security for ten years. What I can say is that, since 1996, we've spent \$800 million to improve Johannesburg alone. I'd like all those who keep repeating that our cities are dangerous to reflect on conditions in their own metropolises. What interests me is the security of the sporting event. From this point of view, I'd like to point out that in the 11 events we have organised since 1994, we haven't had a single incident. Not one. Our organisers are security experts. As for health, South Africa has a system that can compete with the best in the world. We don't feel second to anybody. People have been coming here for heart transplants since 1960 and our doctors are in demand everywhere. We have world class hospital facilities and great experience in the field of sports medicine, so much so that we host the International Olympic Committee anti-doping lab.'

The statistics unfortunately speak of 5.3 million cases of Aids recorded in South Africa in 2002, with 90,000 newborn babies infected by their own mothers in the same year. In the Rainbow Nation more people die of gunshot wounds than in car accidents and there were more than 22,000 cases of murder in 2000 alone. It is not easy to establish how far these figures will influence the decision of the 24 FIFA delegates. A few weeks ago, welcoming the South African president Thabo Mbeki to Germany, chancellor Gerhard Schroeder promised his country's support for South Africa. In the meantime, Danny Jordaan is still travelling without respite. His charisma, his contacts and his political clout play in South Africa's favour. It remains to be seen whether he will be able to win this match on his own.
Corriere della Sera, March 7, 2004

The vote was eventually held in Zurich on May 15, 2004. As in Soccer City eight years before, I was there to see Nelson Mandela raise a trophy. Then it was the African Cup of Nations his national team had just won; in Zurich it was his country's right to organise the World Cup finals. In Switzerland as in Soccer City, they were two exciting, lively, unforgettable days. The chaotic heat of Johannesburg, the cosmic cold of Zurich. Joining the two experiences together were the warmth of Madiba's embrace and smile.

South Africa and Morocco have never been so far apart. Today the two African countries clash over the organisation of the 2010 World Cup, the first ever to be held on the continent, after months of expensive and gruelling electoral campaigning to win the preference of 24 voters from six continents (in the event of parity, the FIFA president Joseph Blatter will cast the deciding vote). Of the other candidates, Tunisia have dropped out, and Libya and Egypt have no chance. South Africa are counting on Africa, Morocco on Europe.

The Rainbow Nation's presentation was highly political, featuring a long speech by premier Thabo Mbeki on the concepts of democracy, Panafrican unity, dignity and progress.

Morocco opted to prop up the bridge that ideally links them to Europe. It is only a few minutes' ferry ride from Tangiers to Spain and the Moroccans saw this as their trump card in convincing Europeans how they would feel at home at a World Cup in Morocco. South Africa took five black people onto the stage at the World Trade Centre in Zurich. They were led by Nelson Mandela who, after showing pictures of wild animals, handed the mike to the Ghanaian Abedi Pelé. On behalf of his mates George Weah (Liberia) and Roger Milla (Cameroon), he pointed to the way to follow: South Africa represents Africa, black Africa, the real Africa.

Morocco were accompanied by the former Spanish premier Felipe Gonzalez and, in an attempt to boost their seemingly weak link with the rest of the continent, by the Senegalese prime minister Abdoulaye Wade. Nothing could be taken for granted: aside from Tunisia, only Spain and France openly sided with Morocco. Michel Platini, the French delegate, even went so far as to say that, in the event of a South African victory, he would not take his wife and son to the World Cup, to keep them out of harm's way. South Africa's Achilles heel is its high crime rate and the huge spread of Aids. Paradoxically, the assignment of the World Cup comes exactly a year after the Casablanca terrorist attack that cost the lives of 45 people and Moroccan terrorists were arrested for the train bombings in Madrid.

Four years ago, South Africa lost the 2006 World Cup to Germany by a single vote. The country was ready then and came to Zurich yesterday expecting to win. Its prime minister and as many as three Nobel Peace Prize winners – former presidents De Klerk and Mandela who, from 1990 to 1994, ferried the country from apartheid to its first democratic elections, and archbishop Desmond Tutu – were there to strengthen the bid. 'We are ready and capable, we have desire and passion.' Nelson Mandela, 85, fragile, beaming and as incredibly charismatic as ever, hadn't come all the way to Zurich to see his South Africa lose.

The day after, Madiba's Magic worked.

Nelson Mandela has taken the final significant step on his long walk to freedom. Yesterday in Zurich the man who symbolises all the travails of South Africa lifted the World Cup to the sky. The nation will organise the 2010 World Cup finals, the first ever in Africa. 'The struggle is my life' is one of the famous sayings of the man who spent nearly 26 years, from June 12, 1964, to February 18, 1990, in two South African jails, before becoming South Africa's first democratically elected president in 1994.

'Justice is done,' announced Sepp Blatter, words that sound odd coming from the mouth of the FIFA president, by no means a revolutionary. Blatter, a member of the Olympic Committee that in 1976 ordered the sporting embargo of South Africa (already suspended in 1964) which lasted until 1992, has imposed the principle of the rotation of the World Cup finals by continent and fought hard to take the World Cup to Africa.

Yesterday morning at FIFA House in Zurich it ended 14-10 between South Africa and Morocco at the first round of voting. No one voted for Egypt, Tunisia withdrew and Libya were barred by FIFA following irregularities with their bid. The Swiss, famous for their punctuality, made an exception for Mandela, who arrived ten minutes late. He was welcomed by a huge round of applause as he entered the hall. Then, when Blatter opened the envelope containing the name of South Africa, the party really began, inevitably, with *Shosholoza*, the hymn of South African miners and the symbol of the fight against apartheid. Then archbishop Desmond Tutu danced and songs were sung for Mandela.

The Moroccans reacted badly to the defeat, attacking Blatter and issuing a series of bitter, polemical, out of place comments. In Morocco they really believed they would win, but they were forgetting that South Africa had accumulated a lot of credit with FIFA four years earlier when they were robbed of the 2006 World Cup, assigned to Germany in scandalous circumstances. South Africa asked Nelson Mandela to make his last great journey as an ambassador and once again had confirmation of the former premier's incredible power. South Africans call it 'Madiba's Magic'. Silent but uncontainable power. He was smiling yesterday, the former inmate number 46664 in Robben Island jail. The child born in 1918 in a village in the Transkei will be 86 on July 18. In 2010 he'll be 91. 'I feel like a 15-year-old,' was his first comment on the victory. Then he sent a message to his people. 'Humility, no arrogance, great respect for the losers,' he said and, before leaving 'to go dancing', Tutu whispered, 'Very good, Madiba'.

Tutu and Mandela: the winners are colourful African shirts as opposed – symbolically, but not only symbolically – to the pinstripes of the Moroccan delegation. Roger Milla, Abedi Pelé, Kalusha Bwalya: the winners are the symbols of African football, opposed to Just Fontaine, born in Casablanca but glorified by the French national team jersey. In times of war and terrorism, the winners are the three Nobel Peace Prize winners South Africa brought to Switzerland: Mandela, Tutu and the Boer De Klerk, who in 1993 shared the honour with Mandela, his successor at the head of the country.

The winner is Thabo Mbeki, the prime minister, re-elected this year, who in 1999 picked up the baton from Mandela, opposed in Zurich to Mowlay, the brother of King Mohamed VI of Morocco. The winner is Africa, opposed to Europe, shamelessly courted by Morocco. 'We are united,' was another of Nelson Mandela's messages yesterday: it is a necessary one because the Rainbow Nation is struggling to find its own new multiracial identity – on a sporting plane, too.

After all the enthusiasm involved in organising and winning the rugby World Cup (1995) and the African Cup of Nations (1996), many disappointments followed. In two football World Cups, in the rugby World Cups, and even in the cricket World Cup, organised by South Africa last year. The quota system of four blacks per team introduced in rugby has also been a failure. Then there are the problems of Aids, crime and the often brutal infighting for the control of power among blacks.

Nelson Mandela is now about to retire from public life. After so many tough political battles, his long walk to freedom came to an end in the best possible way with a sporting success. Now it is up to his country to carry on, even without Madiba's Magic.
Corriere della Sera, May 16, 2004

Also available

Morbo: The Story of Spanish Football *by Phil Ball*
Morbo is the unique element that gives Spanish football its
special flavour. More than mere rivalry, it is the expression in a
thousand provocative ways of the feeling between clubs divided
by history, language and politics. At its most bitter between
Barcelona and Real Madrid, the same spirit courses through
the uncompromising politics of the Basque Country, hangs
over the divided city of Seville and marks Spain's attitudes
towards its national team. In this new edition of his acclaimed
history, Phil Ball also examines the emerging power centres
of La Coruña and Valencia and weighs up David Beckham's
impact on the morbo in Madrid.
£9.99

Tor! The Story of German Football *by Ulrich Hesse-Lichtenberger*
Tor! (Goal!) traces the extraordinary story of Germany's club
and international football, from the days when it was regarded
as a dangerously foreign pastime, through the horrors of
the Nazi years to postwar triumphs and the crisis of the new
century. *Tor!* challenges the myth that German football is
'predictable' or 'efficient' and brings to life the fascinating
array of characters who shaped it: the betrayed pioneer
Walther Bensemann; the enigmatic genius Sepp Herberger;
the all-conquering Franz Beckenbauer; the modern misfit
Lothar Matthäus. And even the radio commentator Herbert
Zimmermann, whose ecstatic cries of 'Tor!' greeted the
winning goal in the 1954 World Cup final and helped
change a whole nation's view of itself.
£9.99

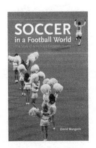

Soccer in a Football World *by David Wangerin*
When the USA reached the 2002 World Cup quarter-finals,
fans had good reason to celebrate. For 100 years they had
been more used to humiliating failures, the repeated collapse
of starry-eyed plans for a pro league and the contempt
of mainstream sports devotees who dubbed soccer "un-
American". Yet the neglected story of American soccer's long
struggle is a rich and surprising one. *Soccer in a Football World*
traces its path from the brief promise of the 1920s, through the
euphoric highs and extravagant follies of the NASL, to today's
hard-won respectability.
£12.99

Visit www.wsc.co.uk to buy and to see our full range of books